Love Is Our Home

Love Is Our Home

THE BEGINNINGS OF THE POST GREEN COMMUNITY

by

Faith Lees with Jeanne Hinton

HODDER AND STOUGHTON
LONDON SYDNEY AUCKLAND TORONTO

British Library Cataloguing in Publication Data

Lees, Faith
Love is our home.
1. Post Green Community
I. Title II. Hinton, Jeanne
267'. 13'0942336   BV4407./

ISBN 0 340 23271 4

First published 1978

Printed in Great Britain for
Hodder and Stoughton Ltd.,
Mill Road, Dunton Green, Sevenoaks, Kent by
C. Nicholls & Company Ltd,
The Philips Park Press, Manchester

"If ever I write the story of Post Green, I'll call it, *No time to die,*" joked Jeanne. "*What a way to die!* would be my choice," I said. Tom overhearing, glanced around at those eating lunch with us, and added teasingly: "How about *Why die for this bunch?*" We all laughed. Later, another fellow-sufferer added his suggestion: "*Lord, just let me die!*"

To all those who have loved, suffered and laughed with us, this book is dedicated.

Foreword

THE COUNTRY HOME of an English baronet and his titled wife might seem the last place to become a vital centre for spiritual renewal for the Church in England. Yet our heavenly Father has many loving surprises for his children, especially when he finds good and honest hearts that are wide open to the leading of his Spirit.

Tom and Faith (as Sir Thomas Lees and Lady Faith would always want to be called) had no formal theological training; yet the Spirit of God found in them a simplicity of faith and willingness to obey – attitudes that often delighted Jesus during his ministry on earth. God may not call many 'of noble birth'; but he calls some, providing they are willing to pay the price of wholehearted discipleship.

To follow the Holy Spirit is always costly, and Tom and Faith soon discovered that their quiet ancestral home in Dorset was being invaded by an ever-increasing number of needy and spiritually hungry people from all over the country. As news spread that God was revealing his love and power in this small but growing fellowship at Post Green, many hundreds came and consequently found their lives transformed, their bodies or minds healed, and their ministries revolutionised by the Spirit. Clearly God was at work, and probably no one was more startled by this than Tom and Faith themselves.

Steadily they learnt to obey the promptings of the Spirit in their own lives, although the demands on their time and energy were not always easy to accept. However, at certain vital stages of development God brought to them those with wider and richer experience, such as Michael Harper, Elmer and Jean Darnall, and Graham Pulkingham. These and others were able to bring them the guidance and encouragement that were needed at different times.

Jeanne Hinton (a journalist who had been working with the Fountain Trust before she joined Post Green) and Faith Lees have written the story with a delightful mixture of humour and honesty. The natural reactions of Tom, Faith and Jeanne to one another and to the great variety of people that God brought to them are described with refreshing candour. This is an account not of super-spiritual saints but of ordinary people with ordinary emotions, genuinely surprised by the gentle and loving invasion of the Spirit of God in their midst.

As such, the book is an immense encouragement to those who want to know more of the reality and power of God. Post Green is a living demonstration that nothing is impossible with God – or with those who believe. Although God has clearly called those at Post Green to work for the renewal of his Church in England, there is no reason why the same Spirit of God should not work equally powerfully amongst all those who are willing to open their lives, relationships and homes to Jesus as Lord.

From the smallest beginnings those living with Tom and Faith have now entered into a deeper, more serious commitment of their lives to one another, as well as to Christ; and in May 1975 the Post Green Community officially came into being. Their vision is "to create an environment where people who have committed themselves to the Lord Jesus can work this out in a loving commitment to one another in such a way that the Holy Spirit can fully use his gifts in their lives . . ." At present they are closely linked with the Community of Celebration, which has sprung from Graham Pulkingham's Church of the Redeemer in Houston, Texas; and God is using them together to bring fresh life and hope to numerous Christians and churches all over the country. It would be hard to read this moving story without receiving a renewed faith in the living Lord who is always doing new things amongst his people.

David Watson
YORK, 1978

Contents

The Stranger

WHEN IT BLOWS a gale on the far northwest coast of Scotland one is foolhardy to venture out without good reason. With little around to break the force of the wind it is not easy to stay upright. It can blow such a gale in the middle of the summer.

"The Old Manse", which my parents had bought and converted into a holiday cottage, is tucked away in a well concealed corner just off the road as it bends out of Scourie village towards Badcall Bay. The centre of the village consisted of one petrol pump, two shops, a handful of small crofting houses, and one hotel for keen fishermen and the more intrepid holiday-maker. Improved roads and a caravan site would follow, but few tourists came that way then.

I was five when my parents first discovered Scourie. Then we stayed at the hotel, my father being an inveterate fisherman. Now married, I came with my own family to stay at "The Old Manse".

Normally we went out whatever the weather, but this particular day we decided it would be better to stay in. We were not expecting any callers. A day or so before the house had been full and the next day more would come, but now there were only Tom and myself, my mother, a friend of my mother's – and oh!, a score of children, my own four, and various nieces and nephews. It was not easy to entertain that many housebound children, so we were glad when evening came. With the children in bed, we settled down for a quiet read. Suddenly, we were surprised by a loud banging on the door.

If it had not been loud we would not have heard the knocking above the whining of the gale. Tom went to the door and I followed him. There in the porch stood a dishevelled, crazy-eyed man. A dark scar ran from the corner of his eye down over his cheekbones. A foreigner by the sound of his voice.

"I'll just ask my wife," I heard Tom say. And he left the man standing there in the porch as he beckoned me back into the sitting room.

There we held a family council with my mother and her friend.

"Have him to stay the night? And with the children here too. You can't! You just can't!" My mother's friend quickly let us know her mind. Her voice rose higher and higher – protesting.

Of course she was right.

Tom went back to tell the man that we were sorry; we couldn't give him a room for the night. He had already tried in the village, he said. We couldn't even suggest other places he could try, for there were none for a further fifteen miles.

When Tom came back into the room, he and I looked at each other and we both looked at my mother.

"It's not exactly what St. Francis would have done, is it?" Tom and I were lay members of the Guild of St. Francis, and Tom voiced what we and my mother were feeling. We were not used to turning people away.

"I think maybe I'll go after him," added Tom.

My mother and I said nothing, but I nodded slightly. We didn't invite further comment from mother's friend.

The man was not on foot; we had noticed a bicycle propped up against the garden wall. Tom, as he turned out of the gate to get into our car wasn't surprised, therefore, that he couldn't see him. But, having reached the hump where our road joins the main one he was more than perplexed not to do so. From that vantage point he could see for some distance both ways.

If the man had decided to try again in the village he would hardly have reached it yet, but as Tom drove there and back he saw no sign of him. He tried the other way without success. He was beginning to feel strangely disquieted; a feeling of failure. When he returned and said that the man was nowhere to be seen he could see I was disturbed too. We both sensed that maybe there was more to this incident than apparent.

It was unlikely that the stranger had turned off the road on such a night. Anyway, there was no cover to be found – just scrubland and marsh. One would still have been able to see him.

I don't know who voiced it first, or why, but we both had the thought at the same moment. What if this caller had been no casual traveller, rather a test to see what we would do?

It was a strange thought.

The next day we made careful enquiries in the village. No one had seen anyone who answered to that description. It seemed he had only called at our house.

Whatever others made of that incident it certainly did something for Tom and me. It is one thing to open one's home to family and friends, but what of "the stranger"?

We were used to offering hospitality; indeed the Lees family had always had a reputation for being hospitable. Tom had never known his home otherwise. Since Tom and I had married there had been few weekends when we had not had other members of the family or friends to stay. Occasionally we invited overseas students from London to spend weekends on the farm. But those who came were always those we chose to invite. Here was someone who had turned up uninvited and at an inappropriate time; a person in need, and we had sent him away. If it had been some sort of test we had not rated well. We vowed to each other then that we would never again lightly say no to anyone who came asking for hospitality.

Whether he sent the man, God must have been listening when we made that vow.

The changes in our life were, at first, hardly perceptible. Up to that point people had come to stay at our invitation mostly because they were our friends and we enjoyed their company; now there were those who came because of some need. They came to our home in the south of England, to Post Green.

One friend was involved in a motor accident. Her husband telephoned to say that she had suffered severe concussion and could she stay with us while convalescing? We said yes, and were amazed at her progress. Then another friend came – having had a hysterectomy – and her recovery was equally rapid; within two weeks she was out on the farm helping to scythe nettles. Married friends wrote after a visit to say how being with us had helped them work through problems in their marriage: problems we didn't know they had. Again, these people we knew; the difference lay in what happened while they were with us.

Other changes took place. Tom and I met people who talked about God healing the sick, and the Holy Spirit empowering us to help those with needs.

As we discovered this power for ourselves, God really began to take us up on our promise to him. Then people began to come in their hundreds because they heard that God was healing people at Lytchett Minster.

2

Maybe I'm Going Mad

THAT INCIDENT WITH the stranger might never have happened, but for my illness some years earlier.

Our family doctor told me I was not sick, but I knew differently. Day after day I had terrible stomach pains. I was unable to sleep at night. I lost my appetite.

"Take a holiday," advised the doctor.

We did, but it made no difference.

Every night I would go to bed at the usual time, but regularly as clockwork I would wake at 2 am cramped with the same pains. Horrid ideas crept in. Perhaps Tom was trying to poison me? Such a thought was enough to convince me that I must be going mad. The sickness was affecting my mind.

I began to despair. There *had* to be something wrong with me physically. The doctor just didn't know; he was wrong in his diagnosis, or he was holding something back, afraid to tell me how ill I really was.

Outwardly I managed to stay reasonably cheerful. If Tom knew of my despair, he said little about it. If he communicated anything it was that the whole affair was a nuisance. I guessed he felt pretty hopeless; what could anyone do when the doctor insisted I wasn't sick?

At night I would try to lie quietly beside Tom, gritting my teeth against the pain when it came. Memories flooded my mind.

Normally I had excellent health. I had always been so sure of myself; always able to do anything I set my mind to. Now the smallest domestic crisis sent me into a frenzy. Outwardly calm, inwardly I would be panicking; my heart beating far faster than it ever should. It was all so ridiculous.

Even when I had been evacuated to Canada during the war and had been so unhappy, I had not been affected like this. Neither by that, nor by the events that followed.

I had resented my parents sending me away and not sending my brother. I was eleven at the time and an aunt in Canada suggested to my parents that they send us children over to stay with her. Andrew, five years older than I, was in the middle of his most important school exams and could not leave. Needing to make a quick decision and certain it was a good thing to do, my parents sent me.

Life pre-war had been the comfortable, affluent world of the late 20s, early 30s; affluent, that is, for some. As a family we were among the wealthy and well-to-do; my child's world captured in the memory of the glossy department store catalogue that I received each year as Christmas approached. A Harrods catalogue. I was allowed to choose my presents – ticking off those I most wanted. The larger items would appear later, gift wrapped; the smaller ones as Christmas stocking fillers.

Until I was five we lived in Sussex, then we moved to Esher in Surrey. My brother Andrew teased me unmercifully and after we moved to Surrey he was aided and abetted by a 15-year-old cousin, Kenneth, and by another younger boy, Nigel, son of one of my mother's friends, both of whom came to live with us. Life thereafter was one of continual scrapping and fierce competition to keep-up-with-the-boys; electric trains soon displacing dolls.

My father worked on the Stock Exchange. Always he arrived home too tired to converse or to play with us. "Be quiet, your father is tired," was a constant admonition. It wasn't until much later, when I was in my twenties and married, that I really began to get to know him and to appreciate him, and that was not long before he died. He was a gentle man, extremely intelligent and at times very amusing, but twelve years older than my mother he seemed – in my earlier days – old indeed, never joining in our more strenuous family pursuits. As well as a keen fisherman he was a gifted watercolour painter; these quieter activities he could engage in away from the clamour of the family.

My mother was a religious woman. She belonged to a movement called the Oxford Group. Group meetings were held regularly in our home and again these were times when we had to be quiet. Rather than sit and make polite conversation with mother's friends I would disappear into the servants' quarters and talk to our two maids. I considered them my best friends. They were young and took me cycling, which I enjoyed.

I relegated God and religion to that part of the adult world that was to me unrelieved boredom. Not all that I learnt from my parents, however, was labelled such. My father collected antiques and he took time to share his interest with us. As a family we regularly visited the London art galleries, my mother taking great pains to read-it-all-up-beforehand, and was gifted in her ability to make the family lecture tour interesting, even entertaining.

When I was seven there had been "the cruise", as it was referred to afterwards in the family. This was a Mediterranean cruise and a big event, but at seven I was rather too young to appreciate it. I remember climbing Vesuvius, how excited I was at the prospect of being able to see inside the big crater, how exasperated at not being allowed to go near the edge. It seemed ridiculous not to do so after climbing all that way. Things I wanted to happen that didn't happen, things I wanted to do that I wasn't allowed to do, are my memories of that holiday. It must have been tiring for the rest of the family.

Throughout my childhood it was the same; invariably I wanted to do something *different*. I did not always get my own way, but as time went on I became more adroit; a habit not easy to break.

When war broke out and the question of Canada arose I made it plain I did not want to go. But this was one occasion when I did not get my own way. It was obvious to me that my parents preferred not to have me at home. After all, life would be a good deal easier and quieter without me.

My Canadian aunt was an eccentric. At first I was a novelty, paraded before all her friends and fussed over, but soon the novelty wore off and I was left severely alone. I did not like to write home that I was unhappy; that my aunt did not think of giving me pocket money and that I was too proud to ask for it. At Christmas I stole – presents to send home to my family.

In high school I was two years ahead of the other girls. Bored, restless and homesick, I excelled in practical jokes. A friend and I would compete to see who could get sent out of the form first, and I usually succeeded. I was, however, intelligent enough for this not to affect my classwork, and by the end of my time there I was still well ahead in my schooling.

Back home my parents had difficulty getting me into school again. In the end I was sent to finishing school. It was more of a club than a school, and at fourteen I was the youngest-to-be-admitted member. Normally one had to be fifteen; they had bent the rules on my behalf.

"And I can only say that we made a wrong decision, Faith."

The headmistress did not seem at all upset at what she had to say to me, rather she seemed glad. Unexpectedly summoned to her study, I was told I was being expelled for troublesome behaviour. I opened my mouth to protest and then thought better of it. My parents had been informed, she said, and would fetch me the next day. I had been there eighteen months and at the end of that school year would be taking Higher School Certificate in English and French. It was no time to be expelled.

I liked the school. At the club we did not have classes, we had lectures. We were left to our own devices as to how we carried out our studies; homework was handed in as and when we did it. But discipline was not so lax that my behaviour in class went unnoticed. It had become a habit with me to play up the teachers, and it was not difficult to get other students to follow suit. There was one teacher, in particular, who had become the constant butt of all our jokes. Possibly it was she who stirred up feeling against me. Ironically, at the beginning of the term I had determined to settle down and to concentrate. I had never had to work hard to pass exams – a last minute shove had usually got me through. This time I had decided to settle down to serious study, but it was not so simple a matter to change overnight from being noisy and wild-spirited. It was too easy to make others laugh, a quick turn of the tongue and it was done.

"Faith, you're so sharp you'll cut yourself," one of my aunts was fond of telling me. If reprimanded by a teacher, a flashing smile and usually all was well.

When my parents came to fetch me I expected them to tell me how upset they were, how I had failed them, what an ungrateful child I was, but they said very little. I arrived home at an inconvenient time. My grandmother, who was staying with us, was dangerously ill. Everyone's attention was on her; there was little for me to do and I had plenty of time to think over what had happened.

Then I overheard my father commenting on the matter.

"I wouldn't let that woman look after my daughter for another day ..."

What was behind that remark?

I wanted to know what had happened when my parents had met and talked with the headmistress. I knew my father had come out of the room very angry. But angry with whom? I rarely saw him angry at all.

By questioning my mother, I learnt a little of how the conversation had gone.

"And I'm afraid the decision is final. We couldn't in any way consider having her back again," the headmistress had said.

Sure of her ground, I can imagine just how surprised she must have been at my father's retort: "Even if you begged me I wouldn't send her back. I feel that you've completely failed to draw out of Faith the things that are in her ..."

Learning of that remark brought me up with a jolt. I

realised how much I had misjudged my parents. They were on my side after all. My bitter feelings at being sent away to Canada were ill-founded; my parents did not love me less or think less of me than they did of my brother.

Even if my parents did not consider I was to blame, I knew that in many ways I had been at fault. If such a thing were to happen again I would have no excuse. I decided then I didn't want to continue to be a bother to people, to my parents in particular.

I resolved to change.

The fact that I had behaved so stupidly posed a problem: what next? I'd missed my chance of taking Higher School Certificate. Now my parents decided to send me to domestic science college in Edinburgh. But for my resolution not to be a bother, I would not have entertained the idea. I wasn't a very domestic person; sailing and outdoor pursuits were what I enjoyed.

When I arrived in Edinburgh I realised that my fears were well-founded. To begin with we had to fill our exercise books with such incredibly fatuous information as "how to wash up a milk jug". My fellow students too were very different from my friends at finishing school.

Even though the war was over by then, conditions were still much the same. We were still rationed, there was little fuel, and it was cold in Edinburgh. The people were stuffy and old-fashioned. It was as well that I had determined to stick it out for my parents' sake. I completed the course and went on to do a further three months' training at the Cordon Bleu School of Cooking in Paris. As a result I became an excellent cook.

That was why he had married me, Tom often said.

If I put my mind to it I could do just about anything I wanted, and make a success of it; that's the way I felt about myself.

Until now.

What *had* happened to me?

I first met Tom at a party in London. This was just before I went to domestic science college in Edinburgh.

"That's the girl I'm going to marry."

Tom had decided that before the end of the evening. An incurable romantic, he still keeps the dress I wore hanging in his wardrobe. We danced together for two hours, but he forgot one small point – to ask my name.

"Who was that girl I was with last night?" he had to ask his cousin Sheena, whose party it had been.

Sheena was my best friend and she saw to it that we met again. She also told me about Tom. The war had been responsible for some startling changes in his life too.

His elder brother had been killed in enemy action just a few weeks before I met Tom. If he had lived his brother James would have inherited the family estate and title, for Tom's father was Colonel Sir John Lees, baronet, with a 2000 acre estate in Dorset. Now, as a second son, Tom would – on his father's death – inherit the estate and title.

That was not all. He had lost an eye while on air crew training in South Africa. He had wanted to be a pilot and with the war just started had joined the RAF as a trainee pilot. But during exercises he had been accidentally shot in the eye by a fellow trainee, which had put an end to all his hopes.

Before going to South Africa he had completed in six months the first year of a degree course in engineering at Cambridge. This was as part of a Royal Air Force Scheme, but with his career in the Air Force at an end there was little point in continuing. He turned his attention to agriculture instead, since now he would be responsible for managing the family estate. When I first met him he had just resumed his studies at Cambridge.

He was the most extraordinary young man I had ever met. Eccentric in dress and appearance, his behaviour matched his looks. He might have stepped right out of a P. G. Wodehouse novel. When I first met him he wore a monocle – he was still getting used to having only one eye – and this added to his exceptionally odd looks. He was a natural clown and had a fund of party tricks. One of his best jokes was his ability to suddenly fall flat on his face from an upright position.

"Look at Tom Lees – drunk again!" someone standing by would be sure to comment to Tom's delight.

He was never drunk, but it amused him to trick people into thinking he was. Usually he did it to liven up some party that might otherwise have flagged. Embarrassed as I often was by his behaviour, it was not long before I decided that he was definitely the nicest of all my male friends.

But I wasn't ready to get married. Tom asked me, but always he received the same answer – no.

I liked Tom, but was I in love with him? It was a question I found hard to answer. I wasn't certain I knew what it was to love someone; perhaps – I thought – I was incapable of loving. But after three years of saying no to Tom, I began to worry that I might lose him if I continued to do so, and I did not want that.

I was seventeen when we met and we were married three years later on March 12, 1949, at St. Peter's, Eaton Square, in London.

Now I had been married nine years. Happily married. And we had four children – Sarah, Christopher, Bridget and Elizabeth; the youngest one year old.

The intervening years had not been easy going, but they had been good years. In the early days of our marriage I helped Tom on the farm, milking the cows, baling hay at harvest time. In the first three years I had three miscarriages, probably because of my unreasonable physical exertions. Being pregnant made little difference to me: I hauled boats about (Tom and I both loved sailing), or shared the heavy work on the farm or in the house. My third miscarriage was a serious one. Four months pregnant, I was told by the doctor that it was possible I was carrying a dead child. For a further two months I continued to carry the baby – dead or alive, I didn't know. At six months it was clear that the baby was dead and the foetus was then removed.

Somehow I took all this in my stride. When eventually I had my first child I considered my miscarriages providential; in retrospect, I considered that at the age of twenty or twenty-one I would not have been a responsible mother.

Not long after Elizabeth was born we moved from Race Farm, our first home, to Post Green. A week before we were due to move, a married friend telephoned. She was also in the throes of moving.

"Faith dear, do you think you could have Mark to stay? There is so much to do and I really don't think I can cope with him and everything."

Mark was her two-year-old. The fact that she couldn't move house and look after one small child struck me as funny.

"Of course we'll have Mark. Actually we're moving too, but that's alright."

What if I did already have four children of my own to consider (one a nursing baby)? What difference would an extra one make? It was a challenge anyway and that was what I liked.

This was a typical reaction on my part. It was the same when Tom unexpectedly brought home three or four extra guests for lunch or dinner (as he often did). I prided myself on being able to manage.

But one thing I had not found so easy. My mother-in-law was partly responsible for this.

One never knew what Tom's mother, Madeline, Lady Lees, would get up to next.

Before the war she ran a girls' school at the Manor where the family then lived. Tom had five sisters and the eldest two were educated at home. They had an excellent governess and as a result Tom's mother agreed to take in several other girls to be educated along with his two sisters. Soon she was running a girls' boarding school and the family moved out during term time to live at Post Green, an adjoining house, moving back into the Manor for the holidays. Madeline Lees' projects tended to have this way of taking over the whole of the family's life.

The war brought the closure of the school, and the Manor was taken over by the army, but it was not long before Tom's mother was into something else.

Short and rather plump, she nevertheless made larger people seem much smaller than she. With her brilliant violet-blue eyes and her inexhaustible good humour she drew people like a magnet. Before people knew where they were they were involved in doing what she wanted them to do. She wanted a lot, I was soon to discover.

For many years she had gathered the children of the village together each Christmas, working with them to present a nativity play. It was always hard work.

"Too much work for one performance that is. Now if somehow we could improve on the performance, capture it on film; well, thousands would see it."

And as far as Tom's mother was concerned they would only have to see the film to become convinced Christians. Like my mother, a deeply religious woman, she could not conceive of anyone remaining an unbeliever once he had been properly presented with the facts about Jesus Christ: his claim to be the Messiah. What an opportunity films provided then for presenting these facts in such a way that thousands would become followers of Jesus Christ! The matter was not to be questioned; it was something we could, and therefore must do.

Some years before she had been to Oberammergau and seen the Passion Play presented there. As a result, she longed to create such a play in England, and now she saw how she would do it – on film. Not just the children of the village, but the whole village could be involved. We would make a film – several films – depicting the life and message of Jesus through the eyes of different characters in the gospel story, starting with John the Baptist.

That we had no experience of film-making was no matter. Obviously people would want to co-operate. She had some foundation for believing that, since people rarely refused to help her; it was not that they were too embarrassed to say no, they preferred to say yes. The cast was gathered: a young man in training for the Methodist ministry as John the Baptist (during term-time he was away studying, so most of the filming had to be done during his vacation); the village doctor as Jesus (6' 7" high, he would stand out from the rest of the cast, an impressive figure with his piercing, deep-set eyes); a young Persian woman as Mary (she had been a pupil at the girls' school run in the Manor – a Moslem, she would be converted to Christianity as a result); a retired insurance agent as Zacharias; a local policeman as a Roman soldier. I was to play the Angel Gabriel, the doctor's two young boys would play Jesus at varying stages of his boyhood – the list was endless, and we would need countless extras for crowd scenes. Ultimately we required a cast of five hundred; considerably more than the population of Lytchett Minster, but others from nearby villages and from Poole and Bournemouth were drawn in.

Filming is an exhausting business. It meant endless hours standing around waiting one's turn and then being willing to do the same thing over and over again. It upset everyone's routine, but it drew the village together in a way that nothing else had done. Farmers offered to do each other's tasks, women who were not needed in a particular scene baby-sat for those who were.

We had been filming three years and were nearing the end when Tom's mother approached me with a request.

"Darling, you know that Roy and I are quite unable to agree about the background music for the film. When it comes to music our taste seems to differ considerably. But this morning when I woke up I thought 'Why, Faith's the person to do it ...'"

Unwittingly, I said yes.

I knew next to nothing about music, nothing at all about putting music to film. Hour after hour was spent in record shops, listening to a bit of one record and then to a bit of another, choosing suitable pieces. Having chosen several I had then to spend more hours, stop watch in hand, finding phrases which fitted the length of the various film sequences.

Finally I was satisfied with what I had put together, but still my mother-in-law and Roy, our director, couldn't agree, either with me or with one another. At this point I was determined that it was my choice or nothing and I used full force to get the matter decided. Having got their agreement I had then to fit music, commentary and film together. With the help of books from the library I pushed on. The result was far better than I or any of us had dared to hope for, but I knew when the job was done that I did feel unusually tired.

But now it was not just tiredness that bothered me, I was sick – very sick; my mind full of frightening thoughts that were still there when morning came and I had to face another day.

3

Taking Things for Granted

MY MOTHER ARRIVED at Post Green one afternoon letter in hand and with a determined look on her face. Since my father's death a few years before she had been living only a mile and a half from us. She accosted Tom.

"You didn't take Faith away for long enough on your last holiday. I have these two places booked at a holiday centre in Devon. Jean and I were going, but now she can't go, and I'd really appreciate it if you and Faith would take our place."

Tom's immediate reaction was to say no, but he hesitated, knowing that my mother was concerned about me.

"Faith's upstairs, I'll ask her," he replied.

She followed him upstairs.

The letter informed us that two rooms were reserved for a holiday houseparty at a place called Lee Abbey in North Devon, a centre for *evangelism* – whatever that meant. It certainly meant something religious.

We looked at each other. Neither of us was inclined to say yes; neither of us liked to refuse outright.

"We'll let you know," we said.

"I really need to write today." My mother always wanted an immediate answer. We acquiesced: we could always write later and cancel.

We didn't. In some way, I was glad to go away – anywhere.

The journey from Lytchett Minster to Lynton in North Devon takes $3\frac{1}{2}$ hours. At any time of the year it is a beautiful drive. But the nearer we got, the more inclined we were to turn back. Just the other side of the Devon border we stopped, needing a drink to boost our morale. It was unlikely that an establishment which existed for the purposes of evangelism would have a bar.

We could, we assured each other, stick anything for just ten days.

What did it matter anyway? All I was conscious of was that my head felt as though it had been bashed against a brick wall times without number. It was raw. My eyes were sore. I ached all over. Yet there was nothing the matter with me, I had been told.

Down Countisbury Hill, below us stretched the water of the Bristol Channel, the little harbour of Lynmouth nestling in the wide sweep of the road as it begins to climb steeply again to the twin village of Lynton. Coming out the other side of Lynton into the dark and sombre shadow of the Valley of the Rocks (where on earth . . . what did it matter?) then suddenly turning a corner and seeing it – a large Victorian house, which could have been stark but which fitted in perfectly with its setting: wooded hills on either side, the late afternoon sun on a glittering sea beyond, the bay at the bottom of a steeply sloping field: a jewel enclosed by high dark cliffs. It was a beautiful spot.

A comfortable twin-bedded room. Out of the window I could see the jagged cliffs. Great cliffs . . . a drop . . . maybe that's where it would all end? Well, what else? What on earth would I do (what would Tom do?) if I were going mad? Or if I had some terrible illness?

Long tables in the dining room, the clatter of cutlery, scraps of conversation. "Where do you come from?" "What do you do?" Not exactly what Tom and I were used to. Only ten days . . . ten days.

After supper, hard-backed chairs placed row upon row in the oak panelled drawing room. A hymn, a word of welcome, another hymn. An elderly clergyman (Jack, they called him) rose to address us.

He didn't speak for long and he spoke quietly and well. The first thing he said was to stick in my mind and I can still remember the intonation with which he spoke.

"I suppose you're all here for recreation. Do you know what recreation means? It means *re*-creation."

Re-creation, a new start, a new birth, re-made. Yes, I needed that, something like that.

I took in Jack's quiet confidence, his low well-modulated voice, the sense of peace he communicated – and began to relax. Perhaps after all we might enjoy this holiday.

We did. My father had taught me years earlier how to paint and for the first time in my life I completed a water colour of which I was actually proud.

Another speaker at the evening epilogue two days later seemed to address me directly.

"Maybe there's some person here who feels they can't cope with their life? Well, the answer is to ask God into your life to cope for you."

That certainly summed up the way I felt. There couldn't be any harm, I thought, in trying it.

That night I prayed my first real prayer.

"God, if you can do anything for me, come into my life and cope please. Because I can't manage by myself."

Two days later I realised that I felt different. Not that I felt any better physically. My head still throbbed and pains continued to cramp my stomach. But, somehow I didn't feel the same person at all. I knew moreover, that there was nothing physically wrong with me. I wasn't ill after all. The doctor had been telling me the truth, he hadn't been lying, hadn't been trying to hide something from me.

It would be a further six months before I was free from physical pain. It would take a while for the message to be relayed from my mind to my body that all was well with me. But I knew without a doubt that all was well. It was this deep down inner certainty that convinced me above everything else of the reality of God himself.

Despite my mother's strong faith and my years of church-going, I hadn't known whether there was a God, why Jesus Christ had to die. Or whether there was any truth in the story that he had risen from the dead. Or, what difference it all made anyway. Tom knew. And his mother certainly knew. I knew that after my marriage and move to Lytchett Minster I had calculated that "to be a good Christian" (which included joining in the affairs of the parish and regular attendance at church on Sunday) was part of my duty as Tom's wife. But I knew that Jesus Christ "wasn't in me". What did it mean anyway to have Jesus Christ "inside one"?

Everyone back home seemed to take their religious beliefs for granted. When I returned from Lee Abbey – obviously different – they were, I am sure, glad. But they were also perplexed. Why did I suddenly have to make such a fuss *about God*?

"Converted? I really don't know what you're talking about, Faith," protested my mother-in-law. "Personally I've never known a time when Jesus Christ wasn't my best friend." It was strange that she of all people found it difficult to understand what had happened to me. But then she had always presumed that all the family knew Jesus as she did.

Her faith was of a very practical kind, as I had realised when we had started making films.

An old Kodak camera had been dug out of the cupboard and put to use. Tom and I had winced at the sight. It was a very old camera, a clockwork one, which had to be wound up by hand. It made a kind of wheezing sound and swayed from side to side on its tripod. Tom's mother had insisted that she knew how to work it.

A week later the family had gathered together to see the results.

"If it was a comedy you were wanting to make, Madeline ..." Tom's father had drily commented, as we blew our noses and stuffed hankies back into our pockets. Nothing, we conceded, is funnier than a really bad amateur film.

"I'm sorry, dear," he went on, as he had leant over to console her. "I know how much you wanted to make a go of this."

I looked at Tom's mother. Her eyes sparked, and not just with amusement.

"You need a lot of expensive equipment to make a good film–not to mention experience." Gerry, Katharine's husband, was frowning.

"And the thing we haven't got at the moment is ready money." Tom's father added a quick reminder.

Tom's mother packed away the cine projector and sat down. It was a deliberate movement to get our attention.

"I believe," she said, "that the Lord will provide."

The rest of us had gone away relieved nonetheless. In our different ways we had all tried to stop her.

A week later Tom's mother called the family together again. "I've got the answer," she told us.

She had discovered that living nearby was a professional film director, Roy Gornold, who had given up a career in the navy to make religious films. She had written to him telling him of her idea, saying that she had a camera, £60 to spend, that she wanted the first scene to run for ten minutes and what would his fee be?

"He and his wife called last night," she said. "Not only would he like to help us himself – giving his services free – but he knows of someone with a film studio who is just about to sell out, and who might be willing to let us have some of his equipment cheaply."

So Roy had become our film director. A charming, quietly spoken man, a committed Christian, Roy was someone in whom Tom's mother had found a kindred spirit. "The Lord will provide," she had said with certainty, and she was right.

There was still the matter of money. Money tied up in land and farming or in stocks is one thing; money readily available to spend another. Family income fluctuated from year to year depending on the weather, farm prices, the stock market ...

"A snack bar!"

The increasing build-up of traffic passing the Manor gates on the main Wareham-Bournemouth road, gave Tom's mother the idea.

"We'll put up a snack bar and serve tea and scones and oh! sandwiches, things like that."

"Perhaps not so much cream, Faith dear." My mother-in-law bent over and whipped some of the cream off the scones right in the face of a startled customer.

As the trained cook in the family I was invaluable, but sometimes too generous.

The snack bar, however, did not make much money. Despite her watchful eye Tom's mother was not a good business-woman.

By the time it was completed the film had cost over £3,000; quite a sum in those days. But always it was "The Lord will provide," and so he did. To help, Tom's mother sold most of her jewellery, exchanged her saloon car for a small mini-van and – after her husband's death (not long after filming had started) – auctioned his collection of vintage port.

To think of the Lord providing or of Jesus Christ being my best friend was a totally new experience for me. I had pestered Tom into attending a service of commitment before we left Lee Abbey. For a man normally so uninhibited he had been strangely embarrassed. I was soon to learn that it was best if I kept quiet about what had happened to me. I didn't always succeed.

The trouble was I had so many questions. What did people mean when they talked about knowing God? How did one become more spiritual?

I got hold of a good many books. I read all about St. Francis of Assisi and St. Teresa of Lisieux and St. Teresa D'Avila. But I still had questions.

Tom got impatient with me. He knew God, but one didn't have to make a song and dance about it.

In South Africa following his accident God had been very real to him. Lying on his hospital bed, restless with pain, Tom was able to think of only one thing: "Why me? Why did this have to happen to *me*?" He was young, he was in the middle of his training to be a pilot ...

"Tom, don't fight this. Accept it."

Someone had spoken, but there was no one there.

It was God speaking to him, he was sure of that. Tom had grown up believing in God, but never had he seemed so close before. Tom knew he needed to do as the voice said, and set himself to obey – to accept what had happened and to go along with it. Almost immediately he felt the difference, the pain lessening.

So Tom knew God, but he took this fact for granted, as he did so many things. With his background it was hard to do otherwise.

Tom's grandfather had moved to Dorset from Lancashire in 1890. Before then the family had lived in Oldham, Lancs, where they owned a cotton mill. James Lees, Tom's great-grandfather, had made the family's fortune. In the 1860s, when most mills closed down because of the cotton famine resulting from the American Civil War, he kept the mill open. It was not in his personal interest to do so, but to close meant that men in his employment would be without work and their families would suffer. In the end the Lees family gained, for when the Civil War ended and there came a boom in the cotton trade their mill was operable, and they benefited as a result.

In 1897, Tom's grandfather, Elliott Lees, was made a baronet for political and public services to the country; he was still at that time Conservative and Unionist M.P. for Birkenhead. He took for his coat of arms the figure of an owl and the words "Without haste, without rest"; apt words for a family described later by Tom's mother in a hastily written family history as "beloved, honest progressive generations; true-to-type, father to son, God-fearing, self-made men right up to the present day."

When the family moved to Dorset they lived at first near Wimborne. Later they bought a large Victorian mansion, South Lytchett Manor, situated in the village of Lytchett Minster, near Poole.

In 1915, Tom's father married Madeline Pelly. Third daughter of Sir Harold and Lady Pelly, she came from an old Dorset family. She was a Red Cross nurse at the time; he with the King's Royal Rifle Corps. (On active service in France and Belgium he was awarded the D.S.O., the Military Cross and the Croix de Guerre for exceptional gallantry). The war over, they settled into the Manor and all seven children were born there: Katharine, James, Rosamund, Anne, Tom, Jane and Mary Gabriel. It was an imposing family to marry into.

One of the first decisions Tom and I had to make after we married was what to do about the Manor house. Having served as the battery headquarters of an anti-aircraft defence regiment during the Second World War it needed a lot of work before it could become a family home once more. Tom's mother and father were still living at Post Green, and all but one of Tom's sisters had married. Did Tom and I want to move into the Manor and make it our home?

I didn't. I knew the family's strong attachment to the house, but I quailed at the thought of running such a large and impractical establishment: what would we do with 29 bedrooms and 13 bathrooms?

"But it's nice for children to have all that space to run around in," Tom told me.

Tom's memories of living in the Manor house were boyhood memories: of exploring little-known rooms and passages; of racing his sisters around the long gallery as they chased from the nursery wing to their parents' bedroom; of playing with the call-pipe that connected his father's dressing room to the butler's pantry; of Friday evenings when the Manor was open house to villagers and they came to dance in the large hall; of winter months when the big house was warmed by log fires and it was one man's full-time job to keep them burning.

But the war had changed much, staffing was not so easy, money scarce. I began to work out what it would cost us to re-decorate and re-furbish as was necessary, all three floors, and stopped after costing just one: the sum was quite impossible. We decided to sell: in time it was bought by the local Council and then became Lytchett Minster Secondary Modern School. Tom and I stayed on at the farmhouse we had first moved into, and ran the dairy farm.

Before his brother's death Tom had had his dream of another kind of life. Thwarted in his ambition to become a pilot he had begun to think instead of emigrating to Canada and farming on the Canadian prairies. With James dead, Tom had put all such thoughts behind him.

He had graduated with a first class degree having completed the third year of his course in only three months, working through the long summer vacation. It had been five years since he had first gone to Cambridge to start his engineering course and he had no desire to prolong the time.

He had impressed the university staff and had been offered a job on the university faculty. It was a tempting offer; he had proved he had a keen mind, and without a doubt he would be exercising it more at a university job than milking cows in Dorset. He was indeed more suited to be a university don than a farmer, but he felt his responsibilities lay now at home; responsibilities he had never anticipated he would have to shoulder.

Indeed most of our memories of those early farming days are of the disasters. There was the afternoon when Tom finished milking only to discover he had left the bung out of the cooler, so that all the milk disappeared down the drain. This was but one incident. There were times when as a family we felt it would pay us to keep Tom out of farming; it was obvious that his ability lay in other areas.

In 1951, two years after we were married, he decided to stand for the County Council as an Independent Candidate. I and Tom's sisters, his mother and other members of the family, canvassed from house to house, addressed envelopes, contributed ideas, made lists. He got in with an easy majority and soon became involved in the area of education, setting up special classes and schools for deprived, subnormal and maladjusted children. Increasingly council work became one of his main areas of interest. In 1951 he also became a Justice of the Peace; at 26, the youngest at that time in the country.

When Tom's father died in 1955, Tom had other responsibilities to carry; responsibilities to family and tenants. "Family" meant not just Tom and I and our children, but his mother, sisters, brothers-in-law, cousins, uncles, aunts, nieces and nephews; all now looked to Tom as head. It included my family too, Tom took that for granted: my mother (particularly since my father had died), her companion, my brother (now married and living in America, but paying us regular visits), my "foster" brothers – all were part of our extended circle. Holidays meant primarily family holidays; all had a blanket invitation to spend a part of the summer with us in Scourie.

"Do you think we should invite my mother to come with us to France?" I would ask Tom, thinking it might be nice to holiday on our own for a change.

"Of course we should invite her," Tom would reply, a little surprised that I had asked.

His new position carried certain other expectations that it would never have occurred to him to question. It had been instilled into him from boyhood that privilege equals responsibility; that it is one's duty to concern oneself with the needs of others, to put that before one's own comfort or pleasure.

As a result, Tom had only to see something needed to be done and inevitably he would offer to do it himself. Fortunately after our move to Post Green we had a farm manager, but Tom still had all the estate to oversee. Before long he was on the Board of Governors of several schools, a member of innumerable committees – all on top of his work on the Council and as a J. P.

I got used to him consulting his diary each morning at breakfast and calmly announcing, "I've got three meetings this morning that I ought to be at. Which shall I attend?"

Then again, in the evening the phone would ring. "We

were just wondering whether to expect Sir Thomas? He was due . . ." I would know that he had double-booked again.

One day he received a letter from the Sea Scouts (as he thought) asking him to be their chairman. As an honorary position it didn't entail anything very arduous, so he wrote back and agreed. Both of us were horrified a little later to discover that he had committed himself to be chairman of the local Sea *Cadets*. This was a very different matter. One involved a few meetings through the year and a general interest in local scouting, the other meant very active participation in leading the cadet corps.

Rather than excuse himself on the grounds that he had made a mistake, Tom threw himself wholeheartedly into the job. For a number of years he was out several nights a week teaching the young cadets seamanship and training their officers to lead. The corps took on a new lease of life as a result, but I found it hard not to resent the time it took up. Was this the most worthwhile way to spend his time? Weren't there others who could do it just as well? The Sea Cadets drew boys who were in many ways underprivileged and poorly educated and this was why Tom spent so much time with them. But I did wish he didn't run his life so haphazardly.

Nevertheless our life was happy as well as full. I had a voluntary job of my own as a hospital librarian, which meant I was out regularly two days a week. After a while I became head librarian, later Deputy County Librarian. There was still time for sailing and parties; at weekends friends came to stay and joined in whatever was going on, even if that meant donning the costume of a Jewish rabbi or a Roman Centurion and taking part in the film-making. (In 1960 we began making a second film: *Messiah*).

If sometimes I questioned our manner of life, it wasn't because I minded hard work. Possibly I needed to see the purpose behind all we did; what we were aiming at. My new found faith in God helped me here.

I wanted so much to tell others what Christ could do for them, but whenever I broached the subject with friends a glassy look would come into their eyes.

Somehow I couldn't convince Tom that we needed to grow more religious, or whatever I wanted. If I had had my way we would have landed up as missionaries in some South American or African jungle. But I knew that Tom would never accept this, or consider any other way of life.

4

I Only Want You to Love

THE YEAR FOLLOWING our visit to Lee Abbey Tom came across a leaflet entitled "Christian Laymen", and was impressed by a reference in it to Christian stewardship: stewardship of time, talents and money.

He was enthusiastic. "Take a look at this. What do you think?" he said, handing me the leaflet.

Tom and I were both members of our Parochial Church Council and Tom had also become a lay reader the previous year. Money was always under discussion at council meetings: we never had enough. Part of the problem was the small congregations in both churches in the parish: the one at Lytchett Minster, the other at Upton, where there were newly developed housing areas and, therefore, a larger population. Our annual income was £600 to be shared between both churches; the amount needed for their upkeep more in the region of £2,000 per annum.

With the Vicar's support, Tom began discovering more about stewardship campaigns. Soon he was in touch with an organisation called Planned Giving Ltd., who said they would be willing to organise a campaign if invited to do so.

"We'll invite the members of the Finance Committee up here and put it to them first," was Tom's next suggestion. When they arrived we served them all with large glasses of rum and orange. Tom wanted them to be in a good mood!

The committee and the P.C.C. were unanimous in their decision to go ahead.

"The first thing you need to do," Planned Giving told us, "is to lay on several good buffet suppers." This was an enticement to people to come and meet their representatives. Tom and I had obviously been on the right lines with our rum and orange.

People came, but neither Tom nor I had anticipated what it might mean for us. We put ten shillings into the church plate each Sunday, and that covered our family's giving. Now we were being told that we should be giving a tenth of our income to the church.

Tom did some quick arithmetic. "Good Lord!" was his immediate response. "I don't think we can afford it."

Some of our income was already pledged to support a number of children other than our own through their schooling; could we afford now to pledge an extra amount to the church? We did some more arithmetic. We calculated that to give away a tenth of our income annually was to give away the cost of a good family holiday abroad. We weren't sure we wanted to do that. We had been told that if we covenanted our giving over a period of seven years the church could recoup the tax on that money. But seven years was a long time to consider: how could we foresee what needs might arise over that period?

We were only just into the campaign and we were the ones being challenged. It was a day or two before we could make up our minds, but in the end we decided to give more than a tenth. If, as a church council we were to raise £2,000 a year by planned giving then it was going to be hard for a lot of people. We were discovering what Christian commitment means.

As a result of this campaign we began to run a street wardens' scheme. We appointed a church representative in each street in the parish: someone to keep an eye on people's needs, be a friend to them. I volunteered to organise this scheme and soon had people appointed for every street. The wardens met together regularly to report progress and to encourage each other.

Gradually we began to notice that more people were coming to church. Within a year our income had risen from £600 per annum to £3,500, considerably more than we had aimed for. We were able to support the founding of a hospital in Basutoland as well as seeing our own needs met.

My involvement with the street wardens' scheme was shortlived: after a while the Vicar decided to organise it himself. He must have felt a little uneasy about me; I was too keen, had too many hairbrained ideas.

I was disappointed, but I knew very well what God was saying to me. I wanted to do some great work for him, but constantly in my mind were the words, "I only want you to love. I only want you to love." I was discovering how one hears God speak. God was telling me that in the first place it was my own family he wanted me to love – he did not want me rushing off here, there and everywhere in a mad effort to serve him.

Once I had thought myself incapable of loving. It was my mother-in-law who had made the difference.

"How *can* you let her?" my mother often exclaimed in amazement when she saw my mother-in-law giving me – as she did most people – enormous bear-like hugs. By my family's standards that was most unconventional, and my mother knew how undemonstrative I was.

Tom's mother hugged just about everyone and when you were hugged by her you experienced an overwhelming sense of being loved. Despite my inhibitions I soon found myself responding and giving her a good affectionate hug back. I longed to love people as she did and being often in her company changed me from being rather reserved and cool to someone who could respond warmly to others. All the family were demonstrative; it was catching.

Now I was being told that this was what God wanted of me – not to seek out people to love, but to love those nearest to me: Tom, my mother-in-law, other members of the family, my own mother, our neighbours.

That was fine, but it wasn't enough.

I had my voluntary work at the hospital and like Tom I became a Justice of the Peace. Husband and wife cannot normally serve on the same Bench; however, any difficulty here was covered by the requirement that we never sat on the Bench at the same time.

I was particularly glad to be made a J.P. As much as I loved Tom's mother it was sometimes hard for me not to compete with her. We were both strong-willed, active women; both liked our own way. But any competition between us was out of the question. It would have made family life unbearable and I soon discovered that I had my own gifts.

After the death of Tom's father there were two Lady Lees, myself and my mother-in-law. I became used to attending public functions and noticing people's disappointment that it was the younger Lady Lees, not the older, who was present. I was glad that I could see the funny side of this, otherwise I might have been more put out. Nevertheless when I became a J.P. I was pleased, partly because here was something she had never done.

Whatever responsibilities I had outside the home, I had to be back by three every afternoon. Tom took this for granted. I was first of all a mother and the children had priority over everything else. Love the children as I might, I found this irksome.

Suddenly I began to feel really trapped. Trapped by my position as Tom's wife and all that entailed. I could see no purpose at all in anything that I was doing – it was nothing, nothing but a round of small, unnecessary activities, with no possibility of change ahead. I felt trapped by the prospect of living in the same place for the rest of my life.

As far as I could I kept these thoughts to myself. I could not tell Tom that I desired to be free of him and of his family and its attendant responsibilities. I lectured myself that I had everything a woman could want: a loving husband, four delightful and healthy children, money, position, a beautiful home and garden. I tried forcing myself to enjoy what I had, but it was unreal. Tom sensed at times that I was unhappy and he was adept at thinking up quick solutions. He would organise a trip into town to buy me new clothes; that is, until he was faced with doing it twice in one week, and that was too much even for Tom. The other answer was always to "try a holiday" and we did that too. We went skiing. But the more Tom tried to please me the more aggravated I became.

I knew I had to resolve the matter. Reading the New Testament while on holiday, I realised how the apostle Paul had been free even when he was in prison and in chains; he had not grumbled or complained about his situation. He saw only an advantage in it; an advantage for the gospel. He acted like a free person. I was seeking freedom too, but I saw I had to discover it within myself, not through a change in circumstances. I sensed God telling me that my escape lay not in running from my responsibilities, but in turning around and heading right into them; seeking to get closer, more deeply involved, not seeking to extricate myself.

It had been only a short-lived rebellion – a matter of a few months, no more – but I had learnt a major lesson in what it means to submit oneself to God and to his will.

I settled down to enjoy life at home. In 1960 Tom was appointed High Sherriff for Dorset (an honorary position, which is held for a year only). This entailed additional entertaining. "I have the best cook in Dorset," Tom would boast. When his listeners came to supper they agreed – although most were surprised to discover I was the cook!

There was much to enjoy. The children were fun, Tom and I loved each other, and I had the kind of home I had always dreamed of having.

Post Green was a large Georgian country house, well-proportioned and elegant. In the eighteenth century it had been a posthouse, a place where the mailcoaches changed horses on the road between Salisbury and Swanage, hence its name. Over the years additions had been built. When Tom and I moved in all the plumbing and wiring needed to be renewed and this was an excuse to sort out a labyrinth of back stairways and passages, replacing them with extra rooms, thus making the house much simpler, lighter and more spacious.

We also began to reshape the garden. We cleared out endless

brambles, extended the lawn to include an old pond which must have been used in years gone by to water the coach horses, developed a woodland area and planted shrubs and bulbs to make it appear natural and unspoiled.

There was something about Post Green itself that helped those who came to stay with us feel rested and at peace. People commented on this often, particularly those who came to stay following the incident in Scourie – that of our unexpected caller.

But I didn't tie up that happening – the promise that Tom and I made as a result – or the events that followed (those who came to convalesce and who made such quick and remarkable recoveries) with my strong desire to be used by God. Gradually I had come to terms with the fact that my life didn't allow me to become an evangelist, a missionary or anything like that. I was a housewife and a mother. We enjoyed ourselves socially, were considered amusing company, were respected in the county for the things we did and stood for, and people enjoyed and benefited from visiting us in our home.

But one day in November 1964 Tom returned from making a telephone call looking distinctly uncomfortable.

5

Only God Could Have Done It

TOM HAD RUNG an acquaintance, and the wife had come to the telephone first. She had not long before undergone a major operation.

"I hope when the surgeon operated he didn't cut out your spirit," Tom joked.

She burst into tears.

Tom had been at a total loss to know what to say next. He stammered an apology; she made a hasty excuse and put down the phone.

"You need to go and see that girl," he said. "There's something wrong there."

I gulped. I wasn't at all sure I wanted to do so, but I knew that now Tom had suggested it I wouldn't feel at peace until I did. Two days later I called on Sally, armed with a half bottle of champagne. Probably she was just suffering from post-operation blues.

When she opened the door I realised that there was more the matter than that. She blurted it out right away. "Thank God, you've come. Jack left me yesterday." She hustled me indoors and poured out the whole story.

She had been suspicious for sometime that Jack was being unfaithful to her, that he was involved with another woman. Now he had left. She had been alone since the previous day, desperate to know what to do.

"What would you do, Faith?" she concluded.

I didn't like to tell her what I thought I would do in similar circumstances. Tom had only to glance at another woman to get a very sharp reprimand from me! There was only one thing I could suggest.

"I think I would ask God to come in and cope in the situation."

Surprised, she replied, "I'm an agnostic. I don't believe in God." She went on talking about Jack, and the various friendships he had struck up with other women over the years. In the end I got her to pack a suitcase and come and stay with us while deciding to what do next.

Tom was out at County Hall when we arrived home; I telephoned and told him what had happened. He returned later to find us sitting either side of the fire in the drawing room, Sally still distraught, I somewhat harassed.

Tom took one look at us and made an amazing statement. "Well, there's no need to worry. There have been too many coincidences already for me not to believe that God's hand is on all this. It'll turn out alright in the end, I promise you."

Horrified, I frowned at him. Did he realise what he was saying? What if it didn't turn out alright? I wanted to stop him saying any more, bolstering up Sally with false hopes. Then another thought struck me: if Tom was going to talk that way to Sally, I had better believe it – for her sake; believe not only that God could, but that he *would* make it alright.

My tummy gave a lurch; I felt excited.

I looked at the others. Sally was still red-eyed and pale, attempting now to smile and to respond to Tom as he chatted on to her about his day. After his first confident statement Tom had left it at that; now he was pouring out drinks for us, asking about the children. Nothing had changed, or had it?

The evening passed uneventfully. Sally repeated to Tom all she had told me earlier in the day and went to bed early. Tom said that next day he would try and meet Jack for a talk.

After Sally had gone I challenged Tom. Did he believe that the situation would work out alright in the end?

He looked a bit nonplussed. "I suppose so. I just said the first thing that came into my head."

"Well, we need to decide now what we are going to believe: either it is or it isn't."

To me it was important to settle the matter. Maybe we needed to take this believing business bit by bit, I suggested; in the first place we could believe that Jack would agree to come and see Sally. Tom agreed.

The following day Tom telephoned Jack and in the evening went off to meet him. He returned with the news that Jack had talked quite openly, had seemed relieved that Tom and I were taking an interest in Sally, but had been quite adamant that he was leaving her. Tom had tried every approach to get Jack to reconsider, but without success. The conversation had reached deadlock when Tom thought to tell Jack about my breakdown some eight years before and how I had been changed through discovering that God could be real in my life.

Jack sat silent, then he got up from his chair, saying, "I'll come over tomorrow at lunch time and see Sally for myself." He made no comment on Tom's story, and they parted soon afterwards.

"I'm not sure," Tom added, "that it's going to do much good."

"What do you mean?" I snapped. "We believed that he would come over and now he is. Of course it's going to do some good." Tom looked surprised at my reaction, but agreed.

I had spent a good bit of that day praying and reading my Bible, trying to think of what to do. "What would Jesus have said? What would he have done?" I questioned. I woke the next morning with the thought in my mind, "When Jack arrives ask him if he would be willing to return just for three months – in order to do the thing a bit more decently."

I was surprised. At first it seemed such a bizarre idea, but as I thought it over I realised that this was a sensible suggestion. For Jack to leave Sally now after she had returned home from a major operation and with Christmas only a few weeks off would hardly help people to think any better of him. Such behaviour would certainly mean his being ostracised by many "county folk". Far better for him if he went about the business of separation in a more discreet fashion.

I was, however, nervous of suggesting this to Jack, and decided to try and see him before he talked with the others. I met him at the door and asked him to take a walk around the garden with me. I knew only one approach.

"I want to put a suggestion to you before you see Sally. Would you consider coming back to her just for three months?" I explained to him why I thought this would be prudent.

His reply was equally direct and to the point.

"That's a very good idea. I'll do that."

I was shaken; I had not expected it to be so easy. However, when we got down to talking things out further with Sally and Jack it was not such easy going. Jack agreed to my proposal but made it perfectly clear it was only for appearance's sake. He was not interested in patching up the marriage. However, he agreed to return in two days' time to talk further, so that he and Sally could begin their three-month-see-the-marriage-out period.

That meant I had two more days to talk with Sally. It seemed strange that Jack should be thinking of leaving her; she was such an extremely beautiful and interesting woman. Now her pride had been badly hurt, and she could not talk about Jack without anger. It was hard to talk of her need to forgive him, to be willing for the sake of their marriage to forego her pride and anger, to do more than a person might conceivably be expected to do in the circumstance. But Sally could sense that events were working out better than she had expected, and gradually accepted that God might be behind it all. She wanted to believe, like Tom, that everything would "turn out alright in the end." As we talked, her natural ebullience reasserted itself.

It was not so easy to stay hopeful when Jack returned. He arrived looking like a thunder cloud; he had not changed his mind about returning temporarily, but he made it plain that it was no joy to him. At supper that night conversation was strained. I attempted to help it along with some of our this-funny-thing-happened-to-us anecdotes, but failed abysmally. Unable to bear it, Sally burst into tears and fled from the room. Tom followed to see what he could do, leaving me with Jack. Once more I came straight to the point.

"Jack, for the last time, will you give up this woman?"

"No, I won't," he shot back, looking distinctly annoyed.

"Alright, but you're going to have to live with this then for the rest of your life. *Will you put your life in God's hands?*"

I was almost shouting at him. His reply was equally forceful: "*Yes, I will.*"

I blinked at him. Did he mean it? As best I could I explained what I thought it meant for him to do this. He nodded in agreement; but at the same time he was looking bemused, as though surprised at himself.

What had happened? I felt awed at how things were going.

I suggested to Jack that we join Tom and Sally in the drawing room and as we walked into the room I announced, "Jack's going to put his life in God's hands."

Tom broke the silence that followed with an uneasy, "Yes, yes, a very good idea. Everyone ought to do that sooner or later."

That was not what I meant. Neither of us were used to talking to people about God in such a direct way, but I knew what I had to do. Nervous, I dared not look at Tom, but I started again more slowly and explained that we should all four get down on our knees and pray together. Since the situation was new to the others too, they meekly did as I said.

I led in prayer using words similar to the ones I had been encouraged to pray in the chapel at Lee Abbey. I heard not only Jack's voice repeating them, but Sally's too.

Sally and Jack left the next morning. "Well, I don't know what all of this means, but I know it means something," was Jack's comment as he got into their car. Privately, he told me that he had not slept all night, but had lain awake with the words, "Those whom God has joined together let no man put asunder," going round and round in his mind. "Not that I've changed my mind about Sally and me," he added. I had not commented any further; I knew that it wasn't my job to press him.

We didn't hear from them for three weeks. It was an unnerving experience: how were they doing? We didn't like to telephone, to appear to be checking up on them. Then Jack rang.

"I thought you'd like to know. I'm back with Sally."

It had happened.

It was the first time we had ever set ourselves to believe God would do something so definite. If we had been wise we would have continued to see Jack and Sally and would have shared with them what little we knew about growing in the Christian life. Tom saw Jack now and again and told me that he and Sally seemed happy enough together. Four years later. I sat next to Jack at a dinner party and he confided, "I don't know whether you'll understand what I mean, Faith, but the only way I can describe what happened to me was that it felt like being born again." I could tell that he was totally unaware that he was using biblical language; he was just searching around for appropriate words.

The marriage stayed together for a further four years, then Sally left Jack. She had got muddled up with another man. Would this have happened if we had cared for them more? Whatever the answer, it was not only Jack's life that had been revolutionised, but also our own – or rather my own.

I no longer felt so content. For years I had longed to help people the way we had managed to help Sally and Jack. Not that we really had done anything at all; we had just followed whatever direction had seemed right to us as we prayed. Now I began to feel restless again. Was this just a random occurrence? From our experience it seemed so, but I wasn't satisfied.

As the months went by I found myself questioning many things, even the existence of God. That shocked me. I held on to the one thing I knew to be true: when I had been sick and had thought of taking my life, I had turned to God for help and been healed.

During this period we paid a second visit to Lee Abbey.

Here we were introduced to a new way of studying the Bible. Each morning guests gathered in the drawing room and a member of the community read a short passage from one of the Gospels, commented briefly and then gave us questions to discuss in small study groups.

"It's a method of studying the Bible you could continue back in your churches," was the suggestion.

We agreed. Tom and I approached the Vicar to ask for his support. "We don't mind if it's only a small group. Those who would be really interested. We wouldn't put pressure on anyone to come unless they really wanted to."

The Vicar was interested, and suggested that we ask a retired Anglican clergyman, the Rev. Baden Ball, who assisted at times at the church, to help lead the studies. A group of fifteen began to meet weekly in our home to study Mark's Gospel.

The first chapter of Mark presented an immediate problem. It mentioned several times that Jesus cast out demons. How were we to interpret such passages?

"Obviously it was their way of explaining what we now know to be some kind of psychological disturbance. Of course no one today believes in the existence of demons as such," Mr Fuller, an insurance clerk, spoke for us all.

"I don't accept that," we were startled by a middle-aged spinster, niece of a Congregational minister. "I believe in demons."

Mabel went on to tell us of missionaries she knew who had returned from overseas and who had some strange stories to tell; *they* said there were such things as demons. It was a new thought to us.

"I really don't see any point in our studying the Bible at all if we're going to pick and choose what we're going to believe," she persisted.

We were not sure how to take that either.

It was not that we all violently disagreed with Mabel; we were just uncertain. Baden wisely said little; he had an open mind about such matters, he said.

In the end Mabel herself resolved what our approach should be.

"I suggest that anything we find too difficult or that we don't understand we put aside, not necessarily feeling we have to make up our minds immediately. By the time we come to the end of the Gospel we may have changed our minds about many things."

That seemed a wise suggestion and we were all happy to leave it like that.

As I spent more time reading my Bible, I found myself thinking often about Mabel's challenge. If I took all I read literally then I still had a lot to learn about God – and to experience.

With the help of Tom's Aunt Mary we began to find some answers.

6

How We Came to Forget the Strawberries

STAYING WITH AUNT Mary at her home in Sussex one chilly October weekend the following year, I picked up a book lying on her kitchen table and began to read it.

Because of my work as a librarian I was constantly on the lookout for new books. This one looked interesting; it had an arresting title, *The Cross and the Switchblade*. Leaning against the kitchen stove for warmth, I flipped through it. It was the story of a preacher to whom some extraordinary things had obviously happened. It was well written. The preacher's adventures had begun when he looked at some pictures of teenage hooligans in a magazine late one night. He had suddenly been gripped by the thought that he needed to go to New York and talk with those boys. I was interested in anyone who got thoughts like that and acted on them.

My reading was interrupted as Aunt Mary came into the kitchen.

"Do you mind if I take this book away with me?" I asked.

I had a great admiration for Aunt Mary. She believed God worked in people's lives. A strong supporter of the Divine Healing Mission in nearby Crowhurst, she would often tell us how people had received healing through prayer. A friend at the Mission had given her the book and she was happy for me to borrow it.

Tom was peering over my shoulder. "Why, that book was mentioned in last month's diocesan newsheet," he said. The

Bishop himself had apparently given it to an enthusiastic review.

Back home there was not much time for reading, but over the next two days I finished it. It was amazing. I read bits out to Tom. "Listen to this. It's rather like what we experienced with Sally and Jack."

The preacher, David Wilkerson, had known God's Spirit telling him what to do in the same direct way we had. Of course, what we had experienced had been on a much smaller scale, but there was a similarity.

Tom read the book too, and found it fascinating.

"I wonder where we can get copies from?" I commented.

"The distributor's name is on the inside cover," he replied. Copies could be obtained from an address in London; an organisation called the Fountain Trust.

"Good Lord, Carol!"

"Faith, what are you doing here?"

In London for the day, I had tracked down the offices of the Fountain Trust. Well, hardly an office, I thought, as I climbed steep stairs to a small private flat. The door was not locked; as I walked in I saw piles of boxes and books stacked in the tiny hallway – this must be the right place. I knocked tentatively on one of the doors off the hallway.

"Come in," a voice said.

Then Carol and I were greeting each other, both equally taken aback. Carol Acworth, a graphic designer, had helped us with continuity for our first film. I had not expected to meet anyone I knew and she was certainly surprised to see me. I explained that I wanted to buy a copy of *The Cross and the Switchblade.*

"I'm sorry, we've completely sold out," was her reply.

I was disappointed. After bothering to find the place (and it had been out of my way) it was annoying news.

A man poked his head around a half open door.

"Suggest some others," he told Carol.

Then he stepped into the room himself. He wore a clerical collar, was otherwise casually dressed, and had an open boyish grin. Before Carol could respond, he picked up some books himself and began to suggest several that he thought would interest me.

"He's the author," Carol told me, as she introduced us.

I looked at the books he had handed me. *As At the Beginning* and *Power for the Body of Christ*, both by Michael Harper.

He was interested that I lived near Poole. Did we sail? He was a keen sailor himself, he explained.

"We sail a lot," I said, adding that any time he was in the area he was welcome to call in.

In the end I left with two books and several brochures, which Michael said would answer any questions I had about the work of the Fountain Trust.

I read the brochures in the train on the way home. The Trust, I learnt, had been founded "to encourage local churches to experience renewal in the Holy Spirit and to recover the full ministry of the Holy Spirit including that of healing."

I picked up *As At the Beginning*. Being a quick reader, I had finished the book by the time the train pulled in at Poole Station.

It told how the modern Pentecostal movement was born in a house on Azusa Street in Los Angeles at the turn of the century. There in 1906 a group of men and women, who had been praying for a religious revival, received what they called "the baptism in the Spirit" and spoke in tongues. They were named Pentecostals because they claimed to have had an experience similar to that of Christians at the first Pentecost.

David Wilkerson in *The Cross and the Switchblade* had also talked of a baptism in the Spirit. He was a Pentecostal minister. The Azusa Street revival had apparently lasted three years and during this time many people had been influenced by it; it had become a worldwide movement, but considered by many a heretical sect.

Now there was a further outbreak of this phenomenon. "A second breath of Pentecostal wind," as Michael called it; people from many denominations claimed that they too had been baptised in the Holy Spirit: Episcopalians, Methodists, Presbyterians, Anglicans, Baptists.

From my reading I gathered that throughout the history of the Christian Church there had been similar occurrences: claims of healings, miracles, speaking in tongues. Inevitably persecution had followed. Those who made such claims were turned out of their churches. Michael Harper was hopeful that this time it would be different, that the movement would be contained within the historic churches – to their advantage.

As I got out of the train at Poole, I was wishing I had talked more to Carol Acworth. What was she doing in the Fountain Trust offices? Had she had this experience? As far as I knew, Tom and I had not met anyone who claimed to have had it.

"Why not ring Pat at Lee Abbey and ask her?" Tom suggested later that evening.

Pat Pilditch at the Lee Abbey Community had become a good friend of ours. I rang her.

Pat was encouraging. Yes, a number of them had read the books and they knew Michael Harper. As a community they were very interested in what was happening. She herself had received the baptism in the Spirit. Had we met Moley and Lionel Osborne, who lived at Harmans Cross, not far from us? We might be able to learn more if we linked up with them.

The next day I drove over to Harmans Cross and introduced myself to the Osbornes. An elderly couple, they were parents of one of the community members at Lee Abbey. I explained why I had come.

"Yes, dear, I'm interested myself," Moley Osborne told me. She was very short, grey-haired and motherly and she had smiling eyes. I warmed to her immediately.

"You see," she went on, "I have two daughters and they both talk of having been filled with the Spirit. Their husbands too. And all four of them are very different as a result. Of course I'm an old lady now, but I'd like to have the same thing happen to me."

Her husband brought us coffee. Less excitable than his wife, he nevertheless sat and nodded his assent to all she had to tell me.

"And," he added, "on Thursday afternoons we have a small meeting here to talk these things over and to pray. We'd be glad for you to join us."

The next Thursday I did. It was not unlike our Bible study group except that at the end there was a time of prayer when people actually prayed out loud in front of each other. It would be a while, I thought, before I would be able to do that.

Tom declined to come to the meeting. Increasingly he had become impatient with my womanly preoccupations, as he called them. He did not mind my going to the Osbornes; indeed he was glad, he said, that I had found people who understood what I was after.

"Perhaps now you'll be easier to live with," he told me. (Neither Tom nor I minced our words with each other.) I did not discuss the matter with him further, but I knew that the time would come when we would have to do so.

In July I met Lucia and Reg East, Moley and Lionel's daughter and son-in-law. Reg was an Anglican clergyman, Vicar of a parish in Essex, and he immediately impressed me as a person Tom would take to. Tom agreed when later I suggested we invite Reg and Lucia to supper.

The day they were due, it had been hot and sultry all afternoon: storm weather. The storm broke just before they arrived; our before-dinner conversation over drinks was punctuated with loud claps of thunder. Soon the rain was pounding against the French windows, obscuring the view. We had to raise our voices to be heard, but conversation was relaxed. Reg and Lucia might have been old friends. I was right, Tom did feel at home with them.

He was, in fact, more impressed than I knew. He couldn't quite put his finger on it, but there was something different about this man, different from other clergymen he'd met. It was like Tom to speak his thoughts out loud.

"What is it that's different about you?" I heard him asking

Reg as we walked through the hall to sit down to supper in the dining room.

"Is there anything different?" was Reg's smiling reply. "If there is, it's probably that I've recently been baptised in the Holy Spirit. That's made quite a difference to me."

"Well, tell me about it," Tom continued, once we had said grace and were ready to start the meal.

Reg produced a pocket New Testament and between mouthfuls of chicken and salad thumbed through several scriptures.

He read us several passages referring to Jesus as "he who will baptise you with the Holy Spirit".

"Jesus is spoken of in the Gospels as the Lamb of God who takes away sin, and also as the one who baptises in the Holy Spirit," Reg explained.

He then turned to the beginning of the Acts of the Apostles and showed how Jesus had told the disciples to wait in Jerusalem until they received power; how he had said to them that "not many days from now you shall be baptised with the Holy Spirit." Then had come the day of Pentecost when they were all filled with the Holy Spirit and spoke in tongues.

"The baptism in the Holy Spirit," Reg emphasised, "is power for service: power to enable us to do the works that Jesus did."

"Can anyone receive it?" was Tom's next question.

In answer to that Reg turned to Luke chapter 11 and read verses 11-12.

"What father among you if his son asks for a fish, will instead of a fish give him a serpent; or if he asks for an egg, will give him a scorpion? If you then, who are evil, know how to give good gifts to your children, how much more will the heavenly Father give the Holy Spirit to those who ask him!"

"It's a matter of asking the Father for what he has promised to give you," Reg explained in closing.

Noticing that the rest of us had almost finished eating, he hastily cleared his own plate. He was not having a very restful meal.

"Well, come on, I'm asking."

Even I was taken unawares by what happened next. I had wanted Tom to receive the baptism in the Holy Spirit, but I was quite unprepared for him to be acting as he was now. He had put down his knife and fork, pushed his plate aside, and was down on his knees beside his chair.

"Let's get on with it then," he said looking at Reg.

I froze. Years of training not to squelch Tom when he was clowning around now came to my aid: I bit back the words on the tip of my tongue. Not that he was clowning now, but why couldn't he have waited until we had finished the meal? I should have warned the Easts. Not that they seemed perturbed. Lucia was laughing.

"Do you want to be prayed for too, Faith?" she asked.

I prized myself from my chair and knelt by the table. I would have preferred to have run from the room.

Reg laid hands on Tom and prayed for him. Tom began to laugh: a deep bellied laugh that caused Lucia to chuckle even more. Reg moved across to pray for me. I was shivering. As Reg prayed, I stopped shivering, but I didn't feel like laughing.

When Tom rose to his feet he was still bubbling with laughter.

"Let's go into the other room and have some coffee," he suggested. He put an arm around Reg and propelled him back into the drawing room, insisting that Lucia follow and that we would think about the washing up later on.

I was glad of an excuse to escape. I busied myself making coffee whilst attempting to pull myself together. As I carried the tray into the drawing room, Tom was recounting how he had felt when Reg prayed for him.

"Like lying back and basking in the feeling of absolute contentment," he said. "I still am," he added, "feeling just happy."

I felt extremely unhappy. I turned to the others, attempting to share with them how I was reacting, trying to make a joke of it. As we talked on I gradually relaxed; by the time Reg and Lucia were ready to leave we were all talking happily about what had happened.

What had happened to Tom, that is.

After they had gone we began to clear away the dishes from the dining room: it was only then that I realised that we had never had our pudding. Two large bowls, one heaped high with strawberries picked fresh from the garden that afternoon, the other full of whipped cream, stood untouched on the serving table.

That night I woke to hear Tom talking in his sleep. It took me a while to realise that he was not speaking in English. He was not talking in any language that I understood, but it was a language. I sat bolt upright. Tom was not asleep at all: he was wide awake and praying – in tongues.

7

What Is Going On?

"WHATEVER'S HAPPENED TO Dud?" Sarah, standing beside me at the tiller, glanced across anxiously. (The children thought it a great joke to call Tom "Dud".)

It was the following weekend and we had sailed from Poole to Lulworth the evening before. Now we were banging up and down in a rough and choppy sea making for Brixham. It was rough enough for me to find myself suddenly jerked off my seat onto the cockpit floor: a hard bump. Still holding onto the tiller, my arm was nearly wrenched off with the effort of holding the boat on course: exhilarating but distinctly uncomfortable.

We had our own boat: a 40ft Bermudan cutter specially built for us. Usually in such circumstances Tom would be barking orders at us all, his temper likely to boil over if we didn't jump to obey. Today his manner had been entirely different; peering into the galley I saw that he was lying on his bunk reading *his Bible*.

"Yes, what has happened to you, Dud?" Chris asked him after supper. "You haven't even complained of feeling seasick today."

Tom described what had happened to him.

"And," he finished, "I think I've been healed of my seasickness."

It was an unexpected bonus, and a lasting one. There was no doubt that Tom had been baptised in the Holy Spirit. I still wanted this baptism, but I did hope that to receive it I wouldn't have to make such an exhibition of myself.

Summer turned to autumn, autumn turned to winter and I was no nearer being filled with the Spirit. Every month we received from the Fountain Trust a magazine called *Renewal* and here I read of a conference they were holding in January at a centre in Hertfordshire. It was over a year since we had come across *The Cross and the Switchblade*. Now we were more knowledgeable about the charismatic renewal, as this neo-pentecostal movement was called, had read several books about the gifts of the Spirit and healing, but still it was all theoretical – to me at least. We booked places for the conference, hoping to learn more.

I knew I wanted power in order to be a more effective Christian, but I was beginning to have questions about "a charismatic experience". My questioning was coloured by the memory of Tom breaking out into tongues the night following his baptism in the Spirit. I had awakened to a flood of strident sound, a cacophony of foreign words literally pouring out of him, a language neither he nor I understood, a stream of unremitting sound; loud and seemingly unending. It had scared me.

The more I read about a pentecostal experience the more nervous I became. I liked what I heard about people being healed and discovering a new love for God and for others, but I didn't want all the trappings that seemed to accompany the baptism in the Spirit.

Moreover, such goings-on were definitely not upper-class. "The pentecostal movement in Britain was to be shaped by plumbers and miners rather than by parsons and country squires," Michael had written in *As At the Beginning*, and I could believe it too. As far as I could make out the present outbreak in the historic churches was mainly among the middle classes. I wondered what certain of our friends would make of it all? Not much, I imagined.

Tom and I were well thought of in the county, and it pleased me. I had wanted our life to be "a success", in the sense that we had done something to earn people's respect; now I was confronted with the possibility of losing face amongst the very people whose good opinion we valued. And what about the children? How would it affect them socially? Would they be cold-shouldered as a result?

I fussed at Tom to weigh these implications seriously before we went to the Fountain Trust conference. A comment he made settled the matter. We were talking about the children and what was best for them, taking a look into the future. We were both well aware of the growing permissiveness in society; we knew we could not protect the children from its influence, nor would it be wise for us to try. We had sought to lay a solid foundation of Christian belief and standards, but was this enough? Tom saw hope in this fresh outbreak of God's power at work in the Church and in the world.

"If God's in it, and I believe he is, and this is the way he is choosing to empower his Church in this generation, then we need to be right in it too – receiving all that there is – for the children's sake, if for no other reason.

"They need all the power that's going if they're to lead Christian lives," he went on. "It's going to be considerably more difficult for them that it has ever been for us. If people think we're foolish then let them."

I did not take much persuading; for all my questioning I saw little hope elsewhere.

"Would you please turn in your Bibles to Judges chapter 6. We're going to be following the story of Gideon ..."

I couldn't remember hearing the story before: how God had delivered the Israelites from the oppression of the Midianites through Gideon and his army of only three hundred. Neither had I ever heard the Bible taught this way. Arthur Wallis, the speaker, created for us a huge, detailed, multi-coloured, three dimensional panoramic picture *with words*, linking the Old Testament to the New and both to the present day. As he drew out the implications of God's directions to Gideon – which resulted in his army being weeded down to just a select few – we saw what God was requiring of us if we would be effective in our turn: forethought, training and self-discipline.

"If you fear to go forward in what God is calling you to do, stop now and think again," Arthur challenged us. "Because it's going to cost you all you have."

Pertinent words in the light of our previous deliberations.

This was Saturday morning, and Arthur was followed by Edgar Trout, a Methodist lay preacher from Devon, who in a very direct and simple way told story after story of people being healed of sicknesses and freed from bondages and fears by the power of the Spirit. I longed to witness these things for myself.

At the end of the day Michael Harper announced a further meeting for those who wanted prayer. Tom decided to go to bed. I stayed.

I sat at the back of the conference lounge and watched Edgar Trout as he moved around the room praying for those who indicated they wanted him to do so. I could overhear some of his conversation with a woman sitting two chairs away.

"You should have written that letter," he told her quietly but firmly.

She was praying, her eyes closed. Now her head shot up, startled by his remark. The look on her face was unmistakably one of "how did you know about that?" She was a stranger to him, how did he know what to say to her? Only God could have told him. As they talked, relief was plain in the woman's eyes, replacing her astonishment.

"It's like watching Jesus." The thought brought a lump to my throat. The way he talked with people, knew what to say to them. One or two wept. That made me feel uncomfortable. "The Lord bless you," he said once or twice as he laid a comforting hand on their heads or shoulders.

He looked tired, this blunt, direct man who spoke in a West Country brogue. A moment or two before one would not have noticed it, but now as he stood and looked round the room he seemed suddenly stooped with weariness. He spoke ponderously: "The Lord's telling me that there's still someone here he wants to bless. Is there anyone else who wants to be prayed for?"

For the moment no one moved. Then a man rose. "Yes, I'd like that."

"Well, brother, it's not you I had in mind, but I'll pray for you." Edgar moved over to him.

Another woman put up her hand.

I had not thought to ask for prayer for myself. Reg had prayed for me to receive the baptism in the Spirit and nothing had happened. And "blessings" were associated in my mind with sobbing. I didn't want to weep in public. It was unlikely any way that I was the person Edgar was looking for.

Now he was praying for the woman who had put up her hand. His eyes swept over the rest of us. "When I came into this room earlier on the Lord spoke to me and said he had brought me here today for one person in particular. Well, I got up at 5 am to get here and now it's late. If the person concerned is too proud to ask for the Lord's blessing that's not my business. I'm sorry, but I'm not going to wait any longer."

"Is it me?" I had to make sure that I wasn't the person responsible for his dilemma.

He looked at me. "Yes, you're the person I'm talking about." He didn't move. I had to get up and go over to him. He indicated we should sit down.

"What's on your mind?"

It was an odd question.

"I don't know. I don't think I have anything on my mind."

He waited, saying nothing.

"I'd like to be filled with the Spirit." It was all I could think to say.

"Why aren't you?"

I thought for a moment. "I suppose I'm not good enough."

"Who is good enough?" he asked.

I had no answer to that one.

"Do you think I'm good enough?" he pressed me.

Put that way, I still didn't have an answer.

"No one can be good enough," he told me, and he sounded a little less fierce as he continued, "it's not possible."

It was the first time I had voiced to anyone my concern that I was not good enough to receive what so many others had received.

"The Lord wants to bless you, sister," he said. And he laid his hands on my head and began to pray for me.

I heard him addressing the fear that was in me, casting it out in the name of Jesus. I didn't burst into tears. I was glad about that. In fact, I didn't feel any different at all.

Edgar was collecting his things, preparing to leave the room. Most people had left now. I sat quiet for a while and then left ahead of Edgar. As I walked away the thought went through my mind, "Next time anyone asks you if you want to speak in tongues, say yes."

That was all.

No one had ever asked me if I wanted to speak in tongues. Nevertheless I was aware the next day that I was half expecting this to happen, could feel myself edging away from those sitting near me in the meetings in case they did. But the subject was never mentioned.

Back home I continued to think out my feelings. I had not thought that speaking in tongues was necessary or important, that it was a gift I wanted or coveted. However, it was called the *gift* of tongues. If any of my friends offered me a gift I wouldn't curtly refuse it; who was I to be arguing with God about which gifts I needed, or didn't need?

"Well, Faith, would you like to speak in tongues?" Stephen Wyatt, a local minster who sometimes led the prayer meeting at Harmans Cross, looked at me enquiringly.

Tom and I had gone to tea with him and his wife. We had been chatting about the High Leigh conference, discussing the people we had met, but the conversation had been general; nothing had been said to lead him to ask that question.

He had interrupted his wife, May, who had been telling us about some of their earlier experiences "in pentecost" as she called it. Not minding, she busied herself removing the remains of our tea while Stephen waited for my answer.

I wished that Tom wasn't present, but I knew what my answer had to be.

"Yes I would," I replied.

The tea cleared, we all knelt and prayed. Stephen talked to me quietly, telling me to open my mouth and to speak whatever words came to mind. Hesitatingly, I spoke a few that sounded odd and jerky, then stopped.

"I have anointed you, and I will anoint you again." Stephen was giving an interpretation of my words.

I had only spoken a few phrases. "You just need to go on speaking out the words that God gives you and believe him. You'll be freer with time," Stephen encouraged me.

Driving back home in the car, I repeated those words over and over again under my breath. I wanted to make sure that I hadn't lost them already.

Two days later, still repeating the same few words, I began to doubt that I could speak in tongues. I was cooking in the kitchen, thinking about this when I heard a car door bang and Diana, a friend from the next village, came hurrying up the path, gesticulating excitedly, a broad grin on her face.

What on earth had happened? I had visited Diana the evening Tom and I had returned from tea with the Wyatts and then she had been far from grinning. Now she looked radiant.

Since her husband had died of cancer eighteen months before, leaving her with three children to bring up, the youngest only two, Diana had been severely depressed, dominated by thoughts of inadequacy, convinced she had failed her husband and that she would in the same way fail her children. I had tried talking to her about God, but she did not see how he could help. Like most people, she wasn't interested in my faith.

I had tried again the other evening; only this time Diana had seemed particularly distressed at my talking at all about God. Unable to decide what exactly I had said to cause her distress, I had thought it best to leave and not to press the matter.

Now, obviously, she had some good news to tell me. In fact, she was in such a rush to do so, she couldn't wait to come into the house. She was motioning to me to pull up the window.

"It's happened, Faith, and it's just like you said," she was calling.

I wrestled the window up.

"What's happened?"

"I've discovered that peace you were telling me about. It was while you were talking to me the other evening ... I began to feel that God was there and that he could help. All you said made sense. I could understand it and I could feel my depression lifting. Well since then I've been praying and reading my Bible and ... well, it's happened."

"That's it!" I thought as Diana drove away, "that's the last time I doubt that God has blessed me."

I needed that encouragement because the next day we received a bad shock.

At High Leigh we had made friends with another woman who suffered from depression. Hers was of longer standing than Diana's; she had been in hospital several times for treatment. She was at the conference with her husband and they were hoping that she would not have to go into hospital again. Tom and I suggested that maybe she could come and spend a few weeks with us at Post Green and that this might help to break the pattern of her depression. We said that we would call on them before the end of the week to discuss the matter further; and so it was on Saturday that we drove to Somerset to visit the couple in their home.

"I took Doris into hospital this morning," the husband told us when we arrived.

We could tell just by looking at him that he had had a harrowing time since we had parted a week before. Three children were at home, two of them noisy and fretful, an elder daughter vainly trying to quieten them whilst attempting to tidy some of the disorder in the house.

The husband took us into the living room and explained that Doris had attempted to stab herself and one of the children. It was not the first time it had happened; she had been violent before. When she was depressed there was no way of ascertaining how she would behave; obviously he had needed to take her into hospital.

"What about the children? Can we do anything for you?" I was asking when the telephone rang.

He went into the hall to answer it. We could hear the children fretting around him and then a different, almost scared note to his voice as we heard him telling them to leave him alone for the moment. He came back into the room and stood for a moment looking blankly at us. Then he pulled himself together and told us: "Doris is dead. Suicide." It didn't seem possible. I opened my mouth to ask questions, then thought better of it.

He was insistent there was nothing we could do. "I'll ring my sister and ask her to come over and get the children." He was politely but firmly hurrying us out of the room and out of the house.

"Do you want to go straight back home?" Tom asked me.

I couldn't think of anything else to do; we couldn't force ourselves on the distraught husband and his three children. I wondered whether we should sit and wait to see if the sister arrived, but it would be difficult if the husband came out and found us just sitting there in our car.

"Yes," I told him.

They were almost the only words we spoke on that drive

home. Twice, thinking we needed to talk out what we were feeling, I opened up the conversation, but there was no response from Tom. That was unlike him. He drove like an automaton, not once did he glance in my direction. I left him alone; we could talk later.

Later Tom was still in this odd wooden state. He made some attempt to join in the conversation at supper, but mostly he was withdrawn and silent. I explained to all four children what had happened; in a crisis they always seemed to know instinctively what to do. They were the ones who carried the conversation.

In bed Tom lay stiff as a board. He had never been this way before. In the morning he would surely have snapped out of it. I lay there praying, thinking about Doris's children and her husband, wondering what would have happened if Doris had returned home with us straight from the conference. Could this tragedy have been prevented?

The next morning Tom was no different.

"What's really up with you?" I wanted to know.

"Nothing."

Mid-morning, I took some coffee to Tom in his study. As I entered the room, I saw him sitting there, his body limp in the chair, his eyes staring. His whole person was faintly reminiscent of ... who? Then I remembered. I could see Doris sitting in a chair in the conference lounge at High Leigh with that same look about her.

"Tom," I said firmly, "we're going to pray together. I'll be back."

The word *oppressed* came suddenly to my mind. I remembered bits of a book that I had been reading that week: *Defeated Enemies* by a Dutch woman, Corrie ten Boom. I needed to look at that book again. It had told how to pray for people in such circumstances.

Shooting down the stairs, I remembered I needed to baste the Sunday joint. My mind was not on what I was doing. As I opened the oven door to take out the joint, I was wondering where I had left the book. I came to with a jerk: what was I doing? I was standing there knife in hand (I had thought I had picked up a spoon) and I was stabbing the joint as if it were a live animal I wanted to kill.

"I'm never going
    to suggest
        we help
            anyone
                ever again."

The words jerked out of me.

"But that's spiritual death!" Even as I realised what I was saying, this other thought flashed through my mind.

Quietly I pushed the joint back in and closed the oven door. I was confident now that I knew what all this was about. Corrie ten Boom had talked about the way evil spirits could influence one. This must be a demonstration of demonic activity.

The book was lying on the table beside my bed and I found the passage. Corrie ten Boom had been speaking at a conference of Bible School students in Japan. She depended upon an interpreter to give her message and the young woman became more and more muddled. Because of her experience in spiritual matters, Corrie discerned the devil at work. She spoke to the spirits.

"Dark power, that hinders that girl from interpreting God's message ... I command you in the name of Jesus to leave her alone. She is meant to be a temple of the Holy Spirit, not your temple."

The girl had then been able to interpret fluently.

I had overcome my previous reluctance to pray aloud in front of people, but I had never addressed spirits before. Back with Tom, I did just this, using similar words.

It worked. Tom was immediately himself again, and we had learnt our first lesson in spiritual warfare. Were these spirits responsible for the tragedy in Doris's life? It seemed likely. There was a lot we still had to learn. We smiled wryly as we remembered how sceptical we – along with others in our

Monday night study group – had been at Mabel's insistence that demons existed.

The following weekend we paid our third visit to Lee Abbey. On our first visit I had come to know God, the second had resulted in our starting a weekly Bible study group in our home. What would happen this time?

We met Nancy.

We sat next to her at breakfast and I noticed she had difficulty slicing the top off her egg. She seemed shortsighted.

"No, I only have one eye, and that's almost blind," she told us.

She looked surprised when Tom told her he had only one eye too. People rarely realised this unless he was wearing his black eye patch.

Tom told her his story, how he had heard God speak to him, telling him not to fight what had happened. Nancy was soon swapping stories about herself. She was almost blind in one eye because she had accidentally sprayed it with caustic soda and as a result developed corneal ulcers. More recently she had been chopping wood and had got a splinter in her good eye, puncturing it. The eye had to be removed.

She told us of her search for God. On her first visit to the eye hospital, following the incident with the caustic soda, she had shared a room with a girl who talked of knowing God. She had been seeking a faith herself, but the girl had not been able to help her, and Nancy had left the hospital feeling even more depressed. Later, however, she had met a member of the Lee Abbey Community and through her visited Lee Abbey and, like myself, had come to know God. She confided that her troubles were still not at an end: she knew she was seriously ill, perhaps incurably so, but the doctors had not been able to identify what was wrong. She suspected cancer.

We liked Nancy. By the end of our stay at Lee Abbey we had become firm friends. We arranged that she should come and stay, and bring her husband, Guy, to meet us. I believed that the Lord could heal her, but this time I was approaching the matter more cautiously.

Nancy came to stay often after that. We hoped that she would feel herself getting stronger. After all, for a number of years now we had experienced God working this way in people, aiding their recovery. Nancy was still convalescing from the operation on her eye, but instead of getting stronger, she seemed to get weaker.

Most of the time she spent in bed. She was by now totally convinced that she would die soon from cancer, and was fearful at the thought. The smallest symptom would cause her to take to bed, and there she would thrash about worried and fretful. I doubted that she was incurably ill, but I knew the pain she felt was real. Unlike Tom who had learned to accept the pain after the removal of his eye, she seemed unable to do so, tensing her body at the slightest spasm.

She had pills from her doctor which helped but often the only way I could get her to relax was by staying with her and comforting her. She would like me to read the Bible to her and when I prayed for her she would often quieten down and sleep. But she never slept for long, soon waking to complain of sickness and discomfort. I spent as much time as I could with her; some nights I slept in the same room. It was then that she was most open to talk about herself and to tell me about her childhood.

She told me about the night her grandmother came to see her. She was seven at the time and earlier that evening she had returned home from an outing with her elder brother and had announced to her family that she had seen a ghost. No one seemed interested, but later that night her grandmother woke her up.

"Come with me," she whispered to Nancy. Nancy had tiptoed excitedly behind her grandmother to her room in another part of the house.

Nancy's grandmother had strange powers; she was a white witch and many people came to her to have their illnesses charmed away. She talked to Nancy about her powers of sorcery.

"These are powers that are passed on from generation to generation," she said. "And I believe you will be the one to inherit them once I am dead."

For a while Nancy revelled in the attentions of her grandmother. As the middle child in the family she often felt left out, but suddenly she was the one who was wanted and who was useful. Her grandmother promised to teach her all she knew. It was exciting being with her, listening to her weird incantations as she worked her spells.

But Nancy had to obey her grandmother implicitly. Increasingly she found she was powerless to do otherwise. Soon she became frightened. One day when she was in her teens she made a little wax image of her grandmother and tried a spell of her own. She stuck pins into the image and prayed that her grandmother would die. She did die, soon after.

"Probably she would have died anyway, she was over eighty," Nancy told me. "But it scared me."

For a while all was well in Nancy's life; the events of those earlier years almost buried and forgotten. There were other things to capture Nancy's attention: at sixteen she met and married her husband, Guy, then a young R.A.F. officer.

This was during the turbulent war years and Guy was often away from home. One evening a gipsy came to her door telling fortunes.

"Because you have wished the death of an old woman nothing will ever go right in your life until something else takes her place," she told Nancy.

"Silly," thought Nancy. "She's just a gipsy."

But from then on unhappiness began to dog her footsteps. Her brother whom she adored was killed in tragic circumstances, likewise a close school friend. At six months their second child developed a brain tumour and died.

All our family loved Nancy. When she was up and about she joined in all we were doing. She was fun to be with and a hard worker, and soon became used to sewing costumes and helping make-up the cast for filming. Seven years and we still hadn't completed *Messiah*. Tom and I gave as much time as we could, but it was never enough.

Tom was by now chairman of the Secondary Education Committee at County Hall, personally responsible for appointing staff to all secondary schools in Dorset. A strong supporter of comprehensive education, he wanted Dorset schools to change to this system, which meant he had to understand and assess new ideas and be able to take decisions that would have far reaching consequences for many people.

Out a good deal of the time, he liked to find me around the house on his return. More and more, however, I was becoming tied to Nancy. To find me time and again closeted away with her in her room was often too much for him. I too sensed that there was little future in this approach. If I believed the Lord would heal her, it was not happening yet.

"What do you make of it all?" I asked Guy on one of his visits.

"Her doctor could tell you better than I could. I suggest you ring him," he replied. Guy seemed reluctant to get drawn into a conversation with me about his wife's illness.

He gave me a number to ring. I rang the doctor and explained who I was.

"There's nothing you can do," was the doctor's discouraging reply. "She's the worst case of self-inflicted injury I know. If she went to a psychiatrist every day for the rest of her life I don't believe she would be healed."

"Is it likely that she has cancer?"

"No, she certainly has not got cancer," he replied.

"For goodness sake don't forget we've got the Jays coming to supper this evening," said Tom one morning as he left for County Hall. From the tone of his voice I gathered that he thought I might well forget. A few minutes before I had gone into Nancy's room and discovered that she had spilled boiling water from her hot water bottle all over herself: I was hurriedly looking for some ointment to soothe her burns.

Later that day Tom, on his way to another appointment, dropped in to see if everything was alright.

"Where's Faith?" he wanted to know. Inevitably I was with Nancy.

Tom's temper rose. The time had come to deal with this situation. The first thing I knew was Tom bursting into the room – pointing at Nancy – exclaiming, "Whatever's got into this woman, I command you in the name of Jesus to get out." Concerned that he was so upset, I hardly took in the words.

As quickly as his temper erupted, it subsided. He too hardly seemed to have noticed what he had said. "I can't stay. Just don't forget supper," he reminded me as he left.

I turned to Nancy. She was fast asleep. I went off to find Bridget and Lizzie and the three of us quickly prepared the evening meal. I was realising the advantages of being a trained cook: it took me very little time to prepare a three course meal for fourteen, and I was adept at utilising whatever help was to hand, whether children or guests.

When I went back to Nancy's room she was awake but looked at me blankly.

"Who are you?" she asked.

Then, "Where am I?"

I was used to the unexpected with Nancy. If she had lost her memory I didn't think it would be for more than an hour or two. I would wait and see what happened. Then if she hadn't recovered, I would ring our doctor.

"Why am I in bed?" she wanted to know next.

"You burnt your side this morning." That seemed the best explanation.

She touched her side gingerly. "Ouch," she said. It was still red and sore.

"I think I'll get up now all the same."

Since I had no desire to discourage her, I helped her to find her clothes and to dress. When Tom returned it was to find Nancy laying the table for dinner.

"I don't know who I am," she greeted him quaintly, "but I understand you're Tom."

It was a week before Nancy recovered her memory, and then the recovery was only partial: she still could not remember anything that had happened over the past three months. Her memory was perfect up to the point when we met at Lee Abbey. After that every memory was blotted out. She remembered nothing of the months of fear and pain. This loss of memory seemed to aid her in building up a different set of reactions to pain. Whereas before a mild headache would have sent her straight back to bed, now she was more in control of herself.

She began to grow in spiritual awareness and understanding in a way she had not been free to do before. Unwittingly, Tom had successfully exorcised whatever spirits had had a hold over her.

She went home, but returned often to stay with us. Nancy could believe now, as she couldn't before, that she was loved and not a failure. Fears that once had crippled her were no longer in control. She began to be able to work out disagreements when they arose between her and another person, not to falsify symptoms in order to get her own way.

Nancy was facing up to life. It was a miracle.

Gradually we were learning more about the healing ministry, stumbling into new areas of knowledge. We were often on the telephone to Edgar Trout in Plymouth asking his advice, and he took to visiting us each time he passed by on his way to and from speaking engagements in other parts of the country. He encouraged us in our walk in the Spirit and shared with us what he saw happening elsewhere in England. Edgar believed that this was only the beginning of a mighty outpouring of God's Spirit upon the Church, and that Spirit-filled Christians needed to be equipped and able to teach others. He had a picture of teaching centres up and down the country to which people could come to learn the same things that he was teaching us: how to follow the leading of the Holy Spirit and how to exercise common sense and discernment. He was as ready to correct as he was to encourage, if he felt that was necessary.

"I have anointed you and I will anoint you again."

I had thought a lot about the interpretation that Stephen had given the afternoon I first spoke in tongues. Was it possible, I wondered, that I had been anointed and filled with the Spirit as Tom and I had believed God would heal the breach in Sally and Jack's marriage? That was when I had felt a definite change take place in me, but I had not been able to identify it.

I asked Edgar if he thought this was possible.

"Yes," he replied. "I think it's very likely."

So, for over two years I had been asking God to give me what I already had. If I had not come into contact with people who were able to teach and encourage me, I would never have discovered how to follow the Spirit and how to open mysel ↑ to receive his gifts. I was beginning to see the importance of teaching in order to make progress in the things of the Spirit.

Edgar was not the only one who helped us. May and Stephen Wyatt had also become good friends. Stephen had a very practical, down-to-earth approach to the Bible. If the Bible said something there could be no doubt of its truth, and if one trusted God and trusted in his word then sooner or later that word would come true. He made everything seem so simple and matter-of-fact and logical. I was a learner and a keen one. Stephen and May would come to tea and Stephen would ask me questions about what I had been reading and thinking; and, like Edgar, if he was doubtful about my answers he never hesitated to say so.

It was on just such a visit that Stephen wandered over to the window, as he and May got up to leave, and looking out over the garden to Poole Harbour in the distance, said "I can see tents ..."

What was he talking about? There were no tents there.

"Yes, tents, many tents ..." he insisted.

Turning to Tom and me with a twinkle in his eyes he added, "You'll be having camps here one of these days!"

"Tents on my lawn. Over my dead body!"

I spoke hotly, and I meant it. I was proud of our garden, though I had less time now for gardening.

We didn't think too much about that incident. But we did wonder about Uncle Fred Andrew's words a little later.

Edgar often gathered his friends together for small teaching conferences at a Christian guest house in Paignton, Devon. It was there we met Uncle Fred. He sat down for tea at the same table and in his rough Dorset burr asked us where we came from.

"Lytchett," said Tom.

We could see he was taken aback.

"What's going on at Lytchett then?" he asked. He started to question us. We could see him getting quieter and quieter as it dawned on him who we were. He lived in the next door village, so he knew our name very well.

"Maybe this is what that vision I had was all about," he ruminated.

One day as he had been driving the local school bus through Lytchett he had seen a vision of the risen Christ: "clear as mud" above the houses in the village.

"Lord, what are you going to do at Lytchett then?" he had asked in his typical conversational way. With Uncle Fred, prayer came so naturally that sometimes it was impossible to tell whom he was talking to: you or the Lord.

As well as being the driver for the school bus, Uncle Fred worked as a chimney sweep. Both were part time occupations; they provided the bread and butter for his family while he got on with his most important work – that of an evangelist. He worked mainly among gipsies; many had been converted through his ministry. It was just like Edgar that he saw the same worth and expended the same energy on encouraging Uncle Fred as he did on us.

We found it thrilling to see God at work. But we were beginning to get repercussions from the family. "Darlings, what *are* you up to?" Anne, Tom's sister, asked when she dropped in unexpectedly one evening.

8

The Letter Jane Found

IT WAS DIFFICULT to explain what was happening; the more difficult because all Tom's family believed in God – in their own way. They were used to hearing his mother talk about the Lord's guidance and provision, but you didn't let religion turn your family life upside down – not in this way. That they found unsettling. Inevitably, whatever Tom did caused ripples throughout the whole family.

We attempted to share what we could with Tom's mother – to explain to her our interest in the charismatic renewal and how we had come to be caught up in it – but she had only one thing on her mind: to get *Messiah* finished.

Our first film, *Voice Crying in the Wilderness*, was already proving a success. In Canada it had been chosen for showing throughout the country, in preference to a £150,000 Hollywood version of the life of Jesus; in India it had been shown to an open-air gathering of some 120,000 people, and plans were already under way for it to be dubbed with Japanese, Persian, French and German sound-tracks. It had been seen by Queen Elizabeth, the Queen Mother, and in Holland by Queen Juliana and Prince Bernhard. Tom's mother was elated; film as a medium for communicating the gospel was everything she had hoped.

However, we anticipated that once *Messiah* was completed she would be captivated by what Tom and I were doing, investigating everything with her usual keenness of mind and enthusiasm of spirit. Whether she would get personally involved we would have to see. But while Nancy was to-ing and fro-ing between us and her home in Plymouth, Tom's mother suddenly and unexpectedly suffered a stroke. Her sister, Lady Alanbrooke, with whom she was staying at the time, rang to tell us and to ask Tom to fetch her home.

It was a shock to all of us to see her on their return, for the stroke had affected her mind and she seemed at first not to know where she was or who we were. Over the following few days she alternated between periods of lucidity, when she recognised us and was able to converse, and periods when she withdrew into another world: half living in the past and half in the present. She complained constantly of severe pains in her head.

We prayed for her to be healed, but both Tom and I wondered whether this was what God would do. She was now 72 years old and we had known for some time life was getting on top of her. She had so many commitments and the filming alone was more than she could cope with; latterly it had seemed harder for her to push on with it. Normally so confident and sure that everything would turn out alright, she had begun to fuss about little things that once would never have bothered her. To most people she appeared the same bright energetic person, but we sensed that underneath she felt differently.

It was during one of the times when she was drifting between her "two worlds" that she mistook Jane, Tom's sister, for me. As Jane entered her room she heard her say, "Oh there you are, Faith darling, I've come to find I have to love you in spite of myself." How much of her inner life was wrapped up in that statement? She must have fought many spiritual battles in order to have stayed so constantly loving and outgoing not only to myself but to others as well. Her personality was such that she was likely to clash with many people, but in all the nineteen years since I had known her we had only had one row. I could not think of any other time when she had shown any anger towards me, or any time when she had been lacking in love. Not that she had hidden the fact that she found me trying at times, but always we had been able to talk about what she was feeling and it had not spoiled our relationship. I knew that in this she was the one who had been the teacher: if she had been otherwise I might have been a much more difficult daughter-in-law. I knew how much I owed to her.

She had been home almost a week, confined to her bed and nursed by her friend Miss Dunkley, with whom she shared her cottage, when Tom and I went across one evening to sit with her. This was one of the occasions when she seemed not to know who we were. We sat, quietly praying in tongues, when we noticed that her eyes, which had been clouded and misty, were bright and clear, and suddenly she spoke in a firm though quiet voice.

"Father, into your hands I commit my spirit," we heard her say. She was quoting words Jesus had said on the Cross, and she spoke as though some urgent struggle had been resolved. "To do with as you will," she added. Then she slept.

Her condition got rapidly worse and she died the following day.

It happened so suddenly that it was hard for us to accept that she had died. It was not possible to imagine life without her. If we had given her more of our time, had not been so busy with our own affairs, would this have happened? Times came to mind when latterly she had asked for my help and I had refused. I wished now that I had not done so; maybe we could have prevented her from getting so exhausted.

For all my dislike of tears, I found myself standing in the kitchen sobbing, as I battled with my thoughts.

"Don't let your hearts be anxious ..." the words from John's Gospel sprang to mind.

They stopped me weeping. As I thought them over I knew God was telling me that this had been his timing, that I was not to take the blame to myself. For her, it was a good thing to have happened.

It was impossible to have met Tom's mother and to have remained indifferent. She was someone "who could have been half-a-dozen things". This was how Mr. Mortimer, the Vicar of Lytchett Minster, put it at her funeral.

"The advice to 'play them one at a time' was wasted breath," he said. Indeed she was someone "whose going deprives us of the most dynamic character many of us will meet and takes one of the strongest wills from among us.

"The stories about her will become embroidered in due time and will be passed on as legends as people recall someone who could – uniquely – arouse both love and exasperation at the same time."

It was a fair summing up.

A little later, while clearing out her mother's papers, Jane came across a comment in a letter to a friend during the time she lived at Post Green: "My constant prayer is that this house should be used for the glory of God."

9

God's Healing People at Lytchett Minster

"I'VE JUST RUNG to tell you we're holding one of our midweek meetings in Poole this coming Wednesday. We've invited an American woman, Mrs. Jean Darnall, to speak. Have you heard of her?"

"Yes, Tom and I met her last weekend at a Fountain Trust conference. I'm glad you've invited her; she seems an interesting person ... Yes ... certainly Tom and I will be there."

Ken Prior was a local Anglican minister. He and another Anglican clergyman, Brian Bell, were themselves baptised in the Spirit and from time to time organised such meetings so that people from local churches could hear of what was happening in the charismatic renewal.

Tom and I had enjoyed hearing Jean speak the previous weekend, but then she had done so only briefly, introducing herself as an ordained minister of the Four Square Gospel Church.

"Preaching Jesus as Saviour, Baptiser, Healer and Deliverer. Four Square – and you can take it from me I was *square*!" she had joked.

As we sat in St. James's Church Hall in Poole we understood more of what she meant.

"I walked into the room," she recounted, "and saw a crowd of people all looking expectantly – *at me*. They were American Episcopalians. But I had walked in on a party, not a meeting. I could see the glasses, and they weren't drinking orange squash either. I blinked to see a young man in clerical dress sitting there quite at home, and was surprised when he waved his pipe at me in a friendly greeting.

" 'I'm sorry,' I said, trying not to look flustered. 'I was looking for ...'

" 'Here we are, Jean.' A face I knew emerged beside me. 'We've been waiting for you ...'

" 'I ... er ... excuse me.' "

Jean had fled to the ladies room in confusion.

In the ladies' room, (she went on to tell us), she took her sermon notes from her handbag and glanced at them nervously. "Six steps towards a Spirit-filled life," she had entitled it, and the first step she had noted down was that God never fills an unclean vessel. One thing she knew for certain: born again Christians did not smoke or drink.

"Lord, what have you got me into?" she wanted to know.

But the only answer that came was the certainty that she had to go back into that room and just see what happened.

Back in the room Jean started nervously, "I think I'll omit my sermon notes and just answer any questions you have," she said.

They had many questions. They had their own stories to tell too. Of how they had come – many of them – to receive the Holy Spirit, and of all that had happened to them as a result.

"Why, having the Holy Spirit inside is like gin in your orange juice!"

Jean swallowed and took a long hard look at the young blonde woman who spoke.

The strange thing to her was they were so sincere and they did talk as though they had received the baptism in the Holy Spirit.

Jean had herself been baptised in the Spirit at the age of fifteen. Previous to that she had been healed of a major attack of kidney poisoning, which threatened her with the possible removal of one kidney. This healing had taken place at a small Pentecostal Mission Church; the family had joined the church as a result. At the age of sixteen Jean had conducted her first healing campaign at a Union Church in West Virginia, and the results had been startling. Later she had gone to Bible college and there she met and married her husband, Elmer. He too had become a minister in the Four Square Gospel Church.

After Bible college, Jean and Elmer had gone as missionaries first to Panama and then to Australia. They then returned to America, Jean to become an assistant pastor at Angelus Temple, headquarters of the Four Square Gospel Church; Elmer to complete his studies for a psychology degree at the Californian State University in Los Angeles. Now Elmer was temporarily in Hong Kong founding a Christian high school and Jean was on a preaching tour of the U.S. and Europe.

"God was teaching me some quick lessons," she told us. "I learned that God does not always work 123456 as I had the steps noted down in my sermon notes, but often his way is 654321."

There had been surprises all along the way for Jean as she travelled throughout the United States and then Europe, talking with Episcopalians, Lutherans, Baptists, Methodists, Anglicans – hearing of what God had been doing and sharing what she too knew. Listening to her excited me; not least, because here was someone who felt as I did about seeing God at work in people's lives. But there were moments when I saw something else too. This woman was tired, very tired.

"Do you think," I said to Tom when the meeting was over, "that she might like to come and spend a day with us? We could make sure she had time to herself and she could rest up a bit."

Tom agreed that I should ask her.

"Thank you, I'd like to," she smiled warmly as she accepted my invitation.

Jean, however, as she confessed to us later, was to regret next morning that she had said yes. She had other things on her mind and could have done without an additional luncheon engagement. At breakfast she asked Ken Prior, with whom she was staying, "Do you think I should go to lunch with these people ... the Lees?" She had consulted her diary to check she had the name right.

"Yes, I think you should go," he encouraged her. Which was not the reply she had hoped for.

I collected Jean from Poole and as we drove back to Post Green she talked about Elmer in Hong Kong, and about Johnny her son who was married and still in the States, and about her teenage daughter, LaDonna, who was travelling with her.

"LaDonna and I are going home in a few months' time via Hong Kong," she said. "We'll meet Elmer there and all travel back to the States together."

"I'd like to hear more of your life back home," I told her.

"I'll tell you later," she promised as we turned into the gate of Post Green. There was a catch in her voice. I saw she was looking at the house, obviously surprised.

"It's Georgian," I explained. "Dates back to the eighteenth century."

Indoors, I left her standing a minute in the hall while I went to find Tom. When I returned she was standing looking at the view, and turning to me she smiled and said softly, "You do have a lovely place to work in. You must love it."

"Yes," I said, "Tom and I consider ourselves very lucky."

"But," she went on, and now she was almost whispering, "where's the lady of the house?"

For a moment I was taken aback and then I realised she probably thought me the maid or the cook. No doubt, in the mêlée of the meeting the previous day I had not introduced myself properly and now here I was standing in the hall in the old blue jeans I often wore. I imagined I did look more like a maid than "the lady of the house".

Laughing I replied, "I am." She looked abashed and then collected herself. What, I wondered, would she think of Tom, who almost certainly was wearing his old green cardigan with the holes in it? Hardly her idea of "an English Lord", as she was later wont to call Tom, wrongly as she knew. As we waited for him, I filled her in on the family and told her how Tom and I had come to experience the power of the Spirit and about our desire to learn more.

Over lunch Jean did share more with us about her life back in California, and told us how she had come to sell her home and most of her possessions before starting out on the present preaching tour.

"Not long after Elmer had gone I found my mind dwelling on a verse in Mark's Gospel. The one where Jesus says to the rich young ruler, 'You lack one thing; go, sell what you have and give to the poor, and you will have treasure in heaven; and come, follow me.' This verse bothered me so much that I included it in a letter tape to Elmer, wrapping it up with news of the children, Johnny in the Air Force and LaDonna at school. 'By the way,' I said to him, and I attempted to sound as casual as I could, 'this scripture has been going over and over in my mind lately. I wonder what it means?'

"If you ever meet Elmer," she smiled at us, "you'll realise he comes to the point quickly. Well I got my reply. 'You know exactly what that scripture in Mark 10:21 says, "Sell everything you have, give the money away to the poor." God must have something to say but you'll never know what the next step is until you've obeyed.'

"So I did," she concluded.

"Sold everything?" I queried.

"Yes," she said. "LaDonna heard the Lord telling her to do the same, even her collection of wooden carved horses that she so loved. What we couldn't sell we gave away. Of course, we kept clothes and things we would need to travel in."

"Not," she said, "that we knew where we were going."

She certainly had our attention now. We waited for her to continue.

"There was another verse that was constantly in my mind too," she went on. "From Isaiah, 'Remember not the former things, nor consider the things of old. Behold, I am doing a new thing; now it springs forth, do you not perceive it? I will make a way in the wilderness and rivers *in the desert.*'

"The day the removal van left the house, a young man, who had just graduated from seminary and started at his first church, telephoned. He rang to remind me that I had promised to hold some services for him once he got settled in to his new appointment. Now I hesitated.

" 'Where is your church, Lee Don?' I said, stalling for time.

" 'Up here in the desert . . .' he replied."

Jean was a born story teller. I could see her standing there in the empty hall of their not large, but once comfortable house, that she and Elmer and the children loved, could picture the look that must have been on her face as she took in those words – "here in the desert".

So she and LaDonna had gone to Lee Don's church at Palm Springs – in the desert. A little church which seated only fifty in contrast to Angelus Temple's five thousand. At Palm Springs Jean had found herself for the first time teaching and ministering to non-Pentecostals – people from many denominations who came seeking the power of the Holy Spirit for themselves. That had been the beginning of the tour which had extended now into Europe.

"Actually, it's LaDonna who's responsible for our being in England at the moment," she told us.

"Oh?" we queried.

"We came over first last October but it was so cold we didn't stay long." Jean gave a rueful grin, as though ashamed. "We left as soon as we could for the continent and were on our way to Italy when we received another letter from Michael Harper inviting us back.

" 'If it was that cold in October, we certainly don't want to be in England in January,' I said to LaDonna. She heartily agreed. But that night she woke me up and said, 'Mama, the Lord has just told me something. We are going back to England and we'll stay there for a while.' "

Jean paused for a moment, then added, "But I'm worried about LaDonna. It's no life for a teenage girl constantly moving around from place to place. At the moment I've left her with friends in Surrey."

Tom flashed a look across the table at me. Then turning to Jean said, "Why don't you both come and stay with us for a while?"

Unknown to Tom and me, Jean had prayed that morning for a better living situation. Not only was she concerned about LaDonna, but she knew how tired she was herself of continually packing and unpacking suitcases. "We need a base for a while," she had said to the Lord.

So Jean and LaDonna came to live with us. Jean did not find it easy to settle. For a few weeks she rested, delighting in the quiet of the Dorset countryside, and at my suggestion she borrowed my oil paints and a canvas and set to painting again ("It's years since I did any ..."). Most weekends, however, she was booked to speak at renewal meetings around the country, and she would return to tell us of people healed and filled with the Spirit, of churches catching a new vision of what their life could be as they listened to and followed the Spirit. But every weekend was not enough for Jean. Soon she began to be restless. It was as though she knew God wanted more of her, but she didn't know how or where to give more. Being restless, however, didn't stop her being fully a part of the family when she was at home. Like Tom's mother, she was a larger-than-life person. When she was around we all had a better time, and if having her to live with us meant more work for everyone (as it did: letters to write, clothes to wash and iron, cases to pack, train schedules to check) it didn't matter because she would return to regale us with more stories of what she had seen God do in people's lives. It was worth it.

"What would ... ?"

"What would you think ... ?"

I had gone to Jean's room to share a thought and we both began to speak at the same time.

I stopped and let her continue.

" ... about having some meetings here?"

The same thought had come to both of us that morning.

Tom and I decided we would talk the matter over with Stephen Wyatt and Ken Prior. Perhaps if we were thinking of holding a series of meetings at which Jean would be the main speaker then it would be best to use a local church for the purpose.

"No," was Ken's advice, "I think more people would come if the meetings were held in a home. How do you both feel about having them at Post Green?"

I smiled. I was remembering when I had turned to May Wyatt saying, "If we could only share what we are experiencing with others – the people who live around here for instance. I wonder how it could be done?"

We were sitting in the drawing room having our usual teatime chat and she had looked up gaily and said – as though it was the easiest thing in the world – "Well, I would start right here – in this room." She and Stephen were great enthusiasts. Now we had our opportunity.

Before our planning had gone very far we received some bad news. Edgar Trout had died of a heart attack. He had just returned home from a particularly arduous series of meetings, and was taken immediately into hospital. He died the following day.

Edgar had known for some time that he was in need of a rest, that his constant travelling and ministry to people in need, was taxing him too hard. But despite advice from his many friends he had not eased up.

What would we do without him? He was a man who was wise where others were sometimes headstrong and foolish; we, like many others, had come to depend on his blunt but discerning counsel. Those with him when he had been taken ill, prayed for his healing. Why, when so many others were being healed, had Edgar died?

Several of Edgar's friends, whom we too had come to know, converged on Post Green, grief stricken at the loss. None of us could make any sense of his unexpected death. A large part of Edgar's ministry had been to those in bondage to Satan through dabbling in the occult. As a result, on a number of occasions he had felt the attacks of Satan upon his life. Was this Satan's latest attempt, and his triumph?

As we were all praying together, Uncle Fred broke out with, "Gorr, I just heard a voice as plain as a pikestaff say, 'I tipped the nest'."

Tom, who had been turning over the pages of his Bible, lighted at that moment on Deuteronomy 32, verse 11. He read it to us: "Like an eagle that stirs up its nest, that flutters over its young, spreading out its wings, catching them, bearing them up on its pinions . . ."

The message was plain. When we shared this with Muriel Trout, Edgar's widow, she wrote back with a bit of country lore: an eagle makes its nest of sharp thorns and then covers it with down for the chicks to lie on. When they are old enough to fly it pulls out the down bit by bit until the nest is so uncomfortable that the young chicks take to the air.

This, then, was part of the reason why God had taken Edgar to himself.

We were learning to fly. We had worked out that we had eight Thursdays before Elmer was due from Hong Kong (Jean had persuaded him to come to England, rather than she and LaDonna going to Hong Kong), so we settled on eight conference days: meetings to be held mornings, afternoons and evenings. That would enable wives to come in the daytime and husbands in the evening if child minding was a problem. In the end we compiled a list of twenty people to whom we sent invitations, and we asked them to invite their friends.

Would anyone come? Tom and I had never organised anything of this sort before. By the first Thursday I felt I would be satisfied if only ten appeared.

As it was, by the time the first morning session was under way forty people were sitting in the drawing room, waiting to hear Jean speak. In the afternoon more people came, and in the evening more still.

> *Praise to the Lord, who doth prosper thy work and*
> *defend thee;*
> *Surely His goodness and mercy here daily attend thee;*
> *Ponder anew*
> *What the Almighty can do*
> *If with His love He befriend thee.*

The hymn ended, Jean picked up her Bible and began to read aloud. She had not read far when suddenly she stopped and exclaimed: "Someone's being healed right now ... over there." She pointed to the side of the room by the fireplace. "Whoever it is, stand up and receive your healing."

A woman in her late thirties stood. I had seen her and her husband before at meetings we had attended in Poole and earlier in the evening I had noticed her coming into the house. Obviously a sick woman, she had been helped out of a car and into the drawing room by her husband and a friend. Now she was standing unaided and no longer looked sick; colour had flowed into her cheeks and she stood there literally *glowing*. There was no other word to describe her. And calm; as though she, at least, had not been taken by surprise. But I hardly had time to collect my thoughts, when I heard Jean saying, "And there's someone over there ..."

I couldn't wait for the meeting to end so that I could find the woman who had stood up. I wanted her to tell me what had happened. After most people had gone home, Tom and I sat either side of her on the sofa and she told us her story.

For some years, Dot told us, she had been suffering from severe bouts of haemorrhaging, and each time this left her in a weakened condition. The bleeding had started after the birth of their second child and had become more severe after the arrival of a third several years later. Sometimes she would be too weak to bend and pick anything off the floor; unable to climb stairs. The doctors had concluded she must have a hysterectomy. But by this time Dot and Roy had met people who told them about the gifts of the Holy Spirit and who talked about Jesus' power to heal. Dot became convinced that she could be healed this way too; she decided against an operation. That had been a while back and she had not got any better.

"But this evening, as we sang that hymn, those words 'Ponder anew, what the Almighty can do,' struck me. Since I couldn't stand to sing like the rest of you, I sat there and thought about those words. And suddenly I knew I was going to be healed.

"And then," she continued, "as Jean took up her Bible and began to read I felt this heat flooding through my body and I began to tingle all over. There was such a feeling of joy inside me. If Jean had not told me to stand I would have stood anyway! I couldn't have remained just sitting there.

"And you can see," she went on, jumping up from the sofa and doing a little jig, "I'm not weak now. I know I'm healed."

We laughed; anyone who could jump up from that particular sofa was not weak. Named the "predicament" by Jean who was on the plumpish side and always had difficulty getting up from it, the sofa was not the kind you could spring from easily.

We talked further with Dot and Roy. The friends they had met who shared with them about the gifts of the Spirit and Jesus healing today had also taught them about the baptism in the Holy Spirit and how they could receive this "power for service" themselves.

"But we've lacked teaching," Roy concluded. "The kind of teaching we've had here tonight is the best thing that's happened to us for a long time. We don't get this teaching in our church, you see, and we've even wondered if perhaps we should leave and go elsewhere.

"Somehow," he went on, "I don't think that's the answer." Neither did we.

By the time the fourth Thursday arrived we were no longer holding meetings in our drawing room; we had moved across the way to the Manor School (the Manor that had once been the Lees' home).

"God is healing at Lytchett Minster," the word got around. And people came. At first we overflowed from the drawing room into the hall and up the stairs, and Jean stood in the doorway so that she could be seen and heard by both groups of people; those in and outside the room. Soon we realised the numbers were going to be too large to accommodate in the house. When we moved across to the school they had risen to around three hundred at the evening meetings.

10

Keep Quiet About it, Mum

"WHY ARE YOU so silent, Sarah?" I asked. "Are you bored with what I'm telling you, or just thoughtful?"

Travelling by train to London with Sarah, I took the opportunity to fill her in on recent events. Away at boarding school, the children were unable to be at the Thursday meetings. I was secretly hoping I could take the matter further with Sarah; perhaps explain how she could open her life to God. While Bridget and Lizzie were excited about what was happening, Sarah and Christopher increasingly made it clear they felt otherwise.

I talked of the man in the next village who had picked up local gossip about God healing people at Lytchett Minster and who had come to investigate for himself; he believed himself healed of angina.* One woman had had a stroke and been given only a week to live: her husband had been at the meetings and had asked us to pray – now she was up and about again, as well as ever.

Sarah listened, but said nothing. Prodded into some response she told me what was on her mind. "To tell you the truth, Mum, I'm sick to death of hearing about it all. It's not that I don't believe what you're saying, I'm just not interested."

I was the one to fall silent then, wondering how to answer? She had not spoken rudely; she had just given me a straight answer.

*Since substantiated

"Well," I said eventually, "which is better, being kept up-to-date, or knowing nothing at all? Which is more helpful?"

"I think, Mum, it would be best if you kept quiet about it," she replied firmly.

We were only a third of the way to London. I had a lot of time to sit and think. When Sarah made up her mind there was no way of budging her.

I remembered how at one time we had thought of Sarah as alarmingly backward. We had been concerned because her only response to our pointing out an interesting tree or flower was a flat, "What tree?", "What flower?" Then one Sunday in church she had turned to me and asked what hymn we were singing. "Look at the hymn board," I told her. "What hymn board?" she questioned, looking blank. It was only fifteen feet away from us. The thought came then that perhaps she was shortsighted, and we hadn't realised it. This was the problem; we were soon to discover that Sarah, rather than being backward, was of above average intelligence. But she always did pretty much as she pleased: "appalling class work, excellent exam results" would appear again and again on her form reports.

I remembered when she had gone away on holiday with friends of ours. It was her first time away from home and progress was monitored by three postcards we received. The first commented, "What a charming person Sarah is"; the second, "Sarah seems to be joining in a bit more now"; the third, "Sarah's quite at home: what a character!" Reading between the lines we feared the worst, and we were right. The last day of the holiday our friends visited Hyde Park in London and when Sarah nagged them into allowing her to take a rowing boat out alone on the Serpentine, they had their first peaceful moment in days. They discovered her rowing ability was almost nil and having managed to get out into the middle of the lake she was totally unable to get back. Happily they left her there rowing round and round in circles: they could hardly believe their good luck.

Yes, I thought, Sarah would make up her mind about the

Lord when it suited her, not when it suited me. Perhaps it was not surprising that she should find it harder than the others to accept the events that were taking place, but then there was Christopher, who was of a more equable temperament – he too was balking. What would we do if they continued to feel this way?

I knew at least that I must not press the matter with Sarah any further, and before the train pulled into Waterloo Station I assured her that I would not attempt to do so.

That evening I told Tom about the conversation and together we considered what to do. We knew we couldn't easily stop the present series of meetings and now we were also committed to running camps as well.

Encouraged by the way the Lord had spoken about holding meetings, Jean had taken the matter further and suggested summer camps.

"Wherever I go," she told us, "I meet people who would benefit from the kind of teaching we are providing for those who live nearby. If we ran camps then people from a distance would come."

In particular, she was concerned for families and young people. Could we, she asked, hold one camp for families and another for young people, eighteen years and over?

A series of eight weekly meetings was one thing: camps another. Tom and I hesitated. While we were discussing the matter I recalled how Stephen had seen tents as he looked out of the drawing room window.

"Perhaps we'd better say yes, then," commented Tom, as he realised the possible significance of that incident. We decided we would hold the camps in the back paddock, which would anyway be more suitable than the front lawn.

The two camps – the one over the Spring Bank Holiday for families and another over August Bank Holiday for young people – would take us almost to the end of the summer. And then? The children's feelings certainly needed to be taken into consideration.

"It's their home. I wouldn't feel happy continuing to use it this way unless all four approve. And want to join in," said Tom.

That was a tall order, but I knew he was right. I felt the same.

How could we help Sarah and Christopher to find God for themselves? When we had weighed up the pros and cons of getting more involved in the charismatic renewal, our decision to go ahead had been partly for the children's sake: their need to receive all that God had for them. Now Tom recalled how Christopher had pointedly left the meal table earlier that week when we had talked over plans for the camps.

"It seems the more we say the less effect it has,' I worried.

Tom came up with an answer. "I think we need to pray, commit them to the Lord and expect him to change them. We need to leave the matter totally in his hands and not try to manoeuvre things ourselves."

I knew he was thinking of an incident the previous week when we had deliberately left Stephen talking with Christopher in the hope that he would be able to talk Christopher round.

"And," he added, "we'll see by the end of the summer where we are with them. Then we'll think about the future."

Keen as I was to reach Sarah and Christopher I was not so eager to involve my mother. Living as she did just $1\frac{1}{2}$ miles from us, we were in daily contact, but in answer to her questions about our activities I said little. I was never very responsive to my mother, feeling that she would have run our lives for us if we allowed her to. She came, however, to our weekly Bible study and she soon picked up enough to make her want to know more. The day she had asked to borrow my copy of *The Cross and the Switchblade*, I knew I would have to share more with her. In fact she had not pushed me to do so, wisely holding her peace. Not long after Jean arrived, she and I were sitting talking together when my mother appeared.

"I'd like you to pray with me if you would," she said to Jean. My mother never beat about the bush. When she wanted something she always came straight to the point. "I'd like to be filled with the Spirit," she continued, "*and to speak in tongues*." She emphasised the latter.

"I'll leave you to it then," I said quickly, and made my escape.

Jean and my mother got on well together. It would be best if I were out of the way, I told myself.

"You know," Jean said to me later, and there was a telling glint in her eyes as she spoke, "I believe your mother must have been filled with the Spirit many years ago. She just needed someone to encourage her to pray in tongues." My mother had done so, and returned home delighted.

Increasingly, we valued her support. Seeing God at work this way reminded her, she said, of her experiences with the Oxford Group some thirty to forty years before – the time, possibly, when she had been filled with the Spirit herself. And gradually, as she and I came to talk more openly with each other, our relationship improved.

My mother was not the only elderly person present at the meetings. Louie, a friend of my mother's, was healed of spondalitis; that is, deterioration of the vertebrae at the base of the spine. One seventy-year old lady, a friend of the Wyatts, went to her doctor for a periodic check-up.

"Why, what's happened to you?" he asked. "Your heart's better, your blood pressure is better, your arthritis is better – what have you been doing all summer?"

Smiling she replied, "I've been attending these meetings . . .

Most often the healings happened as the meetings were in progress and Jean would stop the proceedings and share what she knew the Holy Spirit was doing or wanted to do. Often Jean was very specific in the "words of knowledge" she gave.

"The Lord is straightening out someone's tail bones," she said on one occasion.

God, it transpired, was healing Mary, a friend of Dot and Roy's. While still in her teens, Mary had tripped and fallen down some steps, injuring her spine. Over the years the resulting damage had caused her increasing pain and difficulty. Prior to her coming to the meetings, it had been discovered that her tail bones were tucked right under – presumably as a result of her fall – and this was the cause of her discomfort. She was faced with having them removed. The healing was later verified and an operation unnecessary.

People were not only healed of physical illnesses. At one meeting an elderly man at the back of the room stood up and, as he did so, gave the most enormous sneeze, making everyone jump. None of us knew why this had happened, but the next week he stood up and told us about himself.

"Usually people say I've got a tile loose, but last week all my tiles came off, and light came flooding in," he shared. "I'm a Congregational minister," he went on, "and for years my life had been spoiled by quite irrational fears – fears that I have not been able to control. Last week when I stood up I knew something had happened to me. And it had. I'm a different man."

"He really is different," one of his church members confirmed later.

Lawrie, Mary's husband, came to the meetings in a questioning frame of mind. A churchgoer for fifteen years, he had nevertheless been aware for some time that there was something missing in his faith, a power that should have been there. Now, as a result of what he had seen he said he had "met Jesus. Jesus as for real, and as in the gospels."

He voiced what many experienced. Les Grey, who came with his wife, Dot, and who described himself as a "dyed in the wool Anglican" commented, "It's been like walking into the pages of the New Testament. I can tell you, it's certainly shaken me up . . ."

It had shaken us too. To think that this should be happening in our home.

There were times when I was certain it was all a dream. Then I would be jerked back to reality by some incident, as happened the time I heard Jean say: "Fallen arches . . . someone is being healed of fallen arches."

There was something so basic and real about "fallen arches"; that could be no dream.

"What are fallen arches?" Jean wanted to know later. We got the person concerned to explain.

The Spring Holiday camp came and went. People brought their own tents and camping equipment and camped in the paddock. They cooked for themselves and we provided the basic facilities: hot and cold running water, toilets, a camp shop. It was a small camp – about seventy people in all. Meetings were held in the house and children had their own camp programme.

We sensed that those who came were there not out of curiosity or in search of new experiences, but had come for teaching. Many had already been filled with the Spirit, but like Dot and Roy they didn't know what to do next: how to utilise the power they had received. Those who had been baptised in the Spirit had found that life had got harder not easier, circumstances more trying. Some had expected healing and not received it, most were fighting inner battles they had not known before.

Tom and I knew what they were talking about.

"We're learners," many of them said. "We don't even know how to pray properly." A good number were totally ignorant of what the Bible taught.

The camp over, we viewed the house – and ourselves. The house was in a sorry state. It would be better, we decided, to hold the youth camp meetings in a marquee if available. We were all exhausted. Because of our inexperience, Tom and I had not realised how much was involved in the running of such a camp.

"What we need," we told Jean, "is not just a few odd helpers around but a real team of people working together."

We were already nervous at the thought of a large number

of young people camping together in the paddock. Tom had some experience of Boys' Clubs and he had worked with the Sea Cadets, but a mixed group of young people from all over the country was another matter.

Jean agreed we needed a team of helpers. "But they must be the right people," she added.

How could we find such people?

"The Lord will bring them," Jean was confident. "And I'll keep my eyes open as I travel around."

The first person she decided to invite was Vic Ramsey. He ran a rehabilitation centre for drug addicts in South London. Then there was David Mills, a young Congregational minister from Reading, who had worked a lot with young people. Don Double, a full-time tent evangelist, "just happened" to have a tent of exactly the right size. All three agreed to come with their wives and families: the beginnings of a sizeable team.

There were those who lived locally: Roy and Dot and others. And Jane, Tom's sister. She had been filled with the Spirit earlier on in the summer.

"We need someone we can put in charge of counselling," Jean told us. "I think I know just the person."

She was thinking of Valerie Bessant, a young school-teacher whom she had met earlier in the year. Valerie agreed to come, though nervously admitting, "I've never done anything like this before."

Nervous as most of us were, we were all on site to greet the 150 young people as they arrived for the camp over the August Bank Holiday. Some came on foot, trailing up from the bus stop shouldering tents and heavy rucksacks; others arrived by car, or were brought by parents, who looked a little anxious at leaving their teenage children behind. Vic Ramsay came with a young man in tow, who had "just come to the Lord and got free". Free of drugs, that is. We too showed some parental anxiety when we noticed that Sarah made an immediate bee-line for him. Since Tom and I had relaxed the pressure, Sarah and Christopher had stopped being quite so negative, and had even decided to take part in the youth camp. Now as I watched Sarah talking animatedly to Vic's young man, I found it harder not to fuss. Not only about Sarah, but again over the responsibility of having such a large, heterogeneous group of young people camped in the paddock. However, we had a large enough team to keep an eye on things, I reassured myself.

Our last team member had arrived that morning. Jean had been re-assessing our needs and had come to the conclusion that we needed one extra, experienced man on the team. We had agreed, but none of us could suggest who this might be. It seemed rather late to invite anyone else.

"I'm looking for Jean Darnell." A small stocky man stood on the porch, a Welshman by his accent.

He introduced himself as the Rev. Wynn Lewis and we invited him in.

"I've left my wife and children down at the garage in the village," he said, and went on to explain that they were on their way to Weymouth en route for France and that their car had broken down just as they entered Lytchett Minster. "Apparently it will take a day or so to get it mended," he went on, "and I remembered that Jean was staying here. I wondered if by any chance we could park our caravan in one of your fields overnight?"

A Pentecostal minister from Derby, Wynn Lewis had met Jean at a meeting in London earlier in the year. Now I saw Jean, who had arrived on the scene, viewing him with a grin on her face.

"Why, yes," she answered for us, "you're just the person we want . . ."

I wasn't so sure as I looked at him, summing him up. There were Pentecostals . . . *and Pentecostals*, I was coming to realise. Some pentecostals were alright, and others . . . well, they just wouldn't fit into our kind of set up. I just hoped that Jean knew what she was doing.

For all our weeks of preparation the camp passed in a flash. But memories of it remain fresh and vivid. The eagerness of those young people to learn all they could, their reluctance to leave the tent at the end of a meeting, the extended times of praise and worship that resulted. Standing in the paddock outside the tent at those times, the sense of worship hung lambent like a mantle over the camp: a brilliance one could not actually see and yet it was so tangible – awesome.

Memories of Jane and Valerie walking arm-in-arm across to the counselling tent, confessing their nervousness to each other, neither having prayed before for anyone to be be baptised in the Spirit. And then arriving at the tent to find the Holy Spirit at work. There was nothing for them to do, except later to sit down quietly with these young people and share scriptures with them.

Memories of Christopher being led to the Lord by a young Russian, Tony Timosenko, a member of the camp team, who spoke one evening at one of the meetings – telling how his family had been converted from atheism to Christianity as a result of his father's life being miraculously preserved during fighting in the Second World War; of Bridget, Lizzie and Benita, Jane's daughter, standing in row with other young people, anticipation on their faces as they waited to be filled with the Spirit. And of the evening when Don asked all those who wanted to make a fresh dedication to the Lord to stand up, and every single one of the young people in the tent rising to their feet; Don questioning them that they really understood what was implied, and giving them opportunity to reconsider, only to get the same response.

Fearful as I was of any kind of emotionalism, I found I could accept all this more readily than I would have thought possible. I was aware that something deep was going on in many people: it was happening among the team too. Two of the men who had come to help, both full-time Christian workers, had been at odds with one another for a number of years. Now unexpectedly thrown together again, they experienced God's love working in them, breaking down the barriers. As a result they were once more firm friends.

It was still hard not to fuss about Sarah. Present at most of the meetings, she nevertheless seemed detached from it all.

All the campers had departed and members of the team were saying their goodbyes to Tom and me when I heard Sarah's voice across the room.

"Could I have a word with you?"

She had not been there a moment ago: she must have just come in. I turned to see her disappearing out of the door with Wynn Lewis, the Pentecostal minister. We had already said our goodbyes to Wynn and his family; Sarah had caught him just as he was leaving.

It was Wynn who led her to the Lord and I knew that the Lord was teaching me a lesson at the same time – that I needed to be open to all whom God sent to help us, not to judge people so quickly.

That evening Sarah shared with us an incident during the camp. She had been present when Jean was praying for some of the young people, and Sarah had allowed Jean to pray for her. Not wanting to pressurise her, Jean had prayed for Sarah briefly in tongues and left it at that. Unknown to Jean, the language she had spoken was Italian and Sarah had understood every word. In very simple words, Jean had prayed the Lord's blessing on her in a language Sarah knew well: she was studying it for her A-level exams. This had touched Sarah as nothing else had done. It made her realise that God was the one who was pursuing her, seeking to draw her to himself.

Now she too had said yes to him.

Elmer, Jean's husband, was due to arrive from Hong Kong.

How, Jean wondered, would Elmer take to England – and to us? She believed that the Lord wanted her to stay in England for some time, but would Elmer feel the same? She had been in the country for several months and had got accustomed to English ways. She was learning "what to do and what not to do"; how quickly would Elmer get acclimatised? Would he even want to stay long enough to give it a try?

We didn't know the answer, but we wanted to let him know he was welcome. We painted a large sign and strung it along the bedroom wall:

WELCOME HOME

So then you are no longer strangers and sojourners, but you are fellow citizens with the saints and members of the household of God. Eph. 2:19.

Elmer seemed happy enough on his arrival and delighted with his reception, if a little bemused. There was hardly time to get to know him before we were packed and off to Scourie for our annual family holiday.

Before leaving, however, we had a short time with Jean and Elmer talking about the future.

My mother was asking if she could move from her home at Rest Harrow into the flat at Post Green, which Jean and LaDonna and now Elmer were occupying.

"I would be happy for them to move into Rest Harrow," she said.

That was one possibility. Up in Scourie we had time to ponder and take stock of all that God had done. One thing the summer had certainly shown us: there were many people all over the country eager for teaching.

God had also made it possible for us to continue holding conferences and camps, now that all four children approved.

II

City of Refuge

I WAS DRIVING the children back to school for the autumn term. It was mid-September and a hot haze shimmered over the countryside; the fields pale yellow where the corn had been cut and stacked, some straw still lying waiting to be gathered in. There was the feeling in the air of everything ordered, no worry, no anxiety, God in charge of his creation, as of our lives: past, present and future. It was weather for lying in the sun, pondering such matters: the sun on one's body, one's thoughts warming to the knowledge of his love, his perfect timing in all things.

The whole summer had been this way. Had there been a day when the sun had not been shining? Looking back I could only recall hot sunny days: days filled with light and life and laughter, expectancy and joy.

"Like Rummar Godden's *Greengage Summer*," I said to Sarah, who was sitting beside me.

She nodded, understanding.

It was a book we both loved. In it, Rummar Godden tells the story of a young girl on holiday in France, opening herself for the first time to new experiences and friendships, and so coming into a mature awareness of herself as a person. As the fruit of the greengage tree ripens, so the effect of love and companionship on the young girl is the same as that of sun and warmth on the fruit, causing it to be fully ripe: soft and sweet and succulent.

I glanced at Sarah. Something firm and unshakeable had happened to her. I thought of the others: Christopher and Bridget and Lizzie. In their different ways they each had a peace and an assurance they had not had before. Tom and I had a lot to thank God for.

I thought back to a conversation that he and I had had while on holiday.

"It's not just the teaching that draws people," I had commented, "It's something about the home too. People feel loved.

"I'm beginning to understand," I went on, "that the Holy Spirit takes our natural ability to love and adds to it. Your family has always been a loving family; that's a lot to do with your mother and the way she expressed love. Now we're benefiting from this in a new way: the Holy Spirit is taking our ability to love and using it. Feeling this love is helping people to open up those bits of themselves that they've never allowed anyone to see before; perhaps never even allowed themselves to see."

Valerie Bessant had helped me to realise this. "Seeing God at work during this camp has been a fantastic experience for all of us, Faith," she said on leaving. "Everything has happened so easily and yet the work has been so deep. Having the camp linked to the home has been an important part of it. There's been a sense of rightness about that. We've felt the love, and we've felt part of your family."

I had gone on to share with Tom an idea I had: that we needed to hold regular meetings – not one day midweek, as we had been doing, but over a weekend.

"That will make it worthwhile having people to stay as well, and they can receive teaching and be part of the family.

"What we also need to do," I added, "is encourage others in the area to open their homes in the same way."

Tom agreed, almost too readily. I realised he had his mind on other things, which wasn't surprising since he still had so many responsibilities outside the home. However, when he was around he gave himself wholeheartedly to all that was going on. He worried me nevertheless.

"If we do decide to continue running conferences and camps this way it's going to change a lot of things," I pressed him.

Tom liked things to stay exactly as they had always been: I did not see him taking easily to change. But he didn't seem perturbed.

"Now that all the family are happy, I don't see any reason why we shouldn't carry on; for the moment anyway," he replied.

I had left it at that.

I dropped Sarah, Bridget and Elizabeth at school and began the journey home. We had talked with Jean and Elmer about my idea of a series of weekend conferences, and the need I felt to draw together the local people who had been supporting us in order to share our plans with them. We had set a date to meet with them.

But I had to acknowledge that I was not wholly happy. I was nearing home now, and the nagging feeling I had had on and off for days was with me again, my earlier contentment gone. I was not worried about anything in particular; just the sense that something was wrong. I had to discover what lay behind this feeling.

There had been one moment earlier in the summer when I had had similar qualms.

It had happened the second morning of the Thursday meetings. I had been sitting, taking note of who was present, when Jean had suddenly announced that instead of teaching, as planned, she felt it right to pray with each person in the room.

I had been slightly surprised, but I trusted Jean and did not comment. There were about forty in the room and she started at the back. As she moved from person to person I could see the effect of her words on them. It was like watching Edgar Trout all over again; the Holy Spirit was telling her specifically what to pray for each person. One or two people wept.

I had still not got used to this. As usual, it was seeing people cry that I disliked, and hearing them loudly praising the Lord as some were beginning to do. Was it because it was so "un-English" that I found this so unnerving?

Neither did I want Jean to pray for me in front of other people. I mumbled an excuse to the person next to me and left the room.

I went out into the garden.

"Should I stop Jean?" I wondered.

To calm myself, I stood, as I had many times before, and looked out over the garden to the square Norman tower of the village church in the near distance, and beyond to Poole Harbour – a slither of blue, shadowed by the distant Purbeck Hills. The day was still and warm and promised to be warmer later. The azaleas and rhododendrums were in bloom; red and gold, interspersed with yellow clumps of late daffodils. I took it all in but my thoughts remained in a turmoil.

I thought of members of the family, of friends, who would certainly raise their eyebrows, or worse, if they came into the house now; would anyway when word got around as it was sure to do.

Then I realised that this was indeed what Tom and I had to face seriously. God was impressing on me that our life was going to change *drastically*; that we had to be willing to lose whatever reputation and standing we still had among family and friends.

I wondered whether I was willing.

"Don't worry, my hand's on this."

The thought was unexpected. Was it God speaking to me? reassuring me?

Well, willing or not, I couldn't stay in the garden any longer. Back in the meeting, it was not long before Jean was beside me, praying. Her prayer turned to prophecy.

"You are anxious about the future; worried about what you see happening. But you need not worry: my hand's on this."

I hardly needed any further confirmation.

And mostly during those weeks I hadn't worried. There was too much to enjoy and to praise God for.

Now I was fussing again. Why? I pondered the matter for a number of days. Then the thought came that I was fearful of myself. But that was nonsensical; hardly anything I could share with anyone else.

Tom and I were booked that following weekend to attend a conference at Torbay Court in Devon. Probably I would not have shared even then what I was feeling if Cecil Cousen, one of the conference speakers, had not asked any who were conscious of particular fears to come forward for prayer.

I knew that I needed to do so.

"What is it that you fear?" Cecil asked.

"I don't know," I answered, "except that in some way I'm fearful of myself. I don't understand why."

Cecil prayed. As he did so, I saw myself sitting in a car, my parents beside me. I was being driven away from school: expelled. I felt again as I did then: horribly guilty, ashamed.

I was waiting for them to voice what they must be thinking. But the voice I heard was not theirs, yet one equally familiar. I heard the Holy Spirit say: "You are fearful because you know your ability to influence people. At school you realised the power you had to lead people astray, but you need no longer be afraid of this. Then you were led by your own desires, now you are led by mine."

Although I had not forgotten what had happened to me at fourteen, I did not think about it any longer.

"I doubt I would ever have put the two things together," I said to Tom later, when I told him how worried and fearful I had been. "I'm so relieved that's been sorted out."

The devil doesn't give up so easily. He now tried another tack.

"It's a tower of Babel you're building ..." The thought was persistent.

This time I shared my concern with Tom.

"We're not building anything," he observed, "certainly not a tower of Babel."

Was this true? The ideas I had about what God wanted to

do at Post Green were *big*: bigger anyway than just another series of meetings. I was beginning to see that we needed to supply what most churches lacked: a family atmosphere where people felt loved and cared for, where their faith in God was built up by experiencing him at work in a powerful way. We needed to encourage churches to work towards this. Was this presumptuous?

The day arrived for the local people to gather at Post Green to hear our suggestions. That morning I woke with the words "Ramoth-Gilead, Ramoth-Gilead . . ." going round and round in my mind.

Ramoth-Gilead?

Was it a place? or what? I couldn't remember ever having heard or read of such a place. Making no sense of it, I went on to other matters.

I had, for example, to find time to pray more about what we were going to say that evening. The first opportunity came just before lunch. I washed my hair and was drying it, Bible to hand.

"Ramoth-Gilead." Those words again.

Hurriedly, I went to find my Bible Concordance.

"Ramoth-Gilead," I read, "the first city of refuge that was set up in the wilderness." References were given in Deuteronomy and Kings.

Not a tower of Babel: *a city of refuge*. Not just one home, but many homes: a place where people could come and find rest and refreshment, healing. That was part of what God wanted to do.

"I think it would be good to have one theme running through the series," Jean suggested.

We were sitting in the drawing room that evening: some twenty of us, discussing the proposed series of weekend conferences that would begin in October and continue to June 1969.

I looked at those who had come. The thought of another series of meetings excited them. These were people who enjoyed God, enjoyed loving him and praising him and seeing others come into that same experience. Their love for and enjoyment of each other was obvious too.

"This is what we want to capture and build on," I thought as I listened to the conversation, "the joy and the praise and the love and people's enjoyment of it. All of this coupled with a sustained faith in what God can do. This is the right atmosphere into which to bring people with needs, so that where their faith may be lacking they can draw strength from the faith of others."

All of those who came that evening wanted to continue to play a part. We resolved to meet regularly for prayer, and in between to keep a prayer rota going, so that right throughout the coming conference season every hour from 6 a.m. to 10 p.m. would be covered daily by one or more intercessors who would pray for the meetings, for people to whom we would be ministering, for Jean as she travelled around the country. People offered their help in other ways – in preparing the house for meetings, making tea and coffee, child-minding and talking and praying for people.

And opening their homes so that people coming from a distance could stay over the Friday and Saturday nights?

That was more difficult: most of their homes were too small, they explained. But maybe there were a number of good bed and breakfast places nearby. Perhaps we could circulate a list.

For the most part the ideas put forward were Tom's and mine: mostly mine. Not many of those present seemed to see much beyond another series of meetings. I didn't mention the scriptures I had read that morning: about the city of refuge.

Elmer had decided that it would be a good idea for him and Jean and LaDonna to stay at least another year in England: "to see what the Spirit's going to do." They would move into my mother's house, and would be fully a part of the team we were gathering around us: a team that would support Jean's ministry as well as the conferences at Post Green.

We wanted to be able to fit more people into the house, so that the meetings wouldn't have to be transferred to the school. We found a way of positioning two mirrors to enable the speaker, standing in the doorway of the drawing room, to be seen by those sitting in both dining room and drawing room. This, with people continuing to sit in the hallway and on the stairs, provided space for about two hundred people. A crèche could be run in the nursery.

We drew up our list of local bed and breakfast houses and sent this with conference details to the four hundred people now on our mailing list. A few of our local team offered to have people to stay, but only a few. I reckoned that at a pinch we could have up to twenty people staying at Post Green for a conference weekend if we made use of camp beds and caravans. In particular, we invited people to stay whom we sensed needed to feel our love for them and to experience being part of a family in order to help them open up to the ministry of the Holy Spirit in the teaching and worship.

We had learnt a lot from Nancy, whom we had met at Lee Abbey. After that traumatic time when the spirits had been cast out of her, she had continued to visit us, still depending for a while on our support and encouragement to help her build new patterns of thinking, of acting and of relating to people, particularly to Guy, her husband. Over the months she had grown spiritually, and had come to see herself as a whole person. Then had come the moment when she had realised that to continue a dependent relationship was wrong, and that she needed to break free of us. This she had managed. We still kept in touch, but she didn't need us in the same way any longer.

We longed to see others receive such healing. More and

more we were coming into contact with people who needed this same kind of loving, sustained nurture in their walk in the Spirit. Probably these people too would need to keep coming back for a while, as Nancy had done, before they would be totally able to stand on their own feet.

Rudolph was one such person.

Rudolph was brought to us by Ina Northey, a missionary who had just returned to England from Canada on a three months' holiday. She turned up at one of the early conference weekends, and returned a little later bringing Rudolph with her. He was her cousin; a man in his sixties, he had been an alcoholic for the past thirty-five years. She felt an old Etonian would probably warm to Tom, who had been at Eton himself.

Ina, who hadn't seen her cousin for a number of years, had tracked him down in a London hospital, where he was attempting to break the drinking habit. She had talked to him about Jesus and his power to set a person free from bondages. She did not expect that Rudolph would respond to what she said – "missionary talk" – but she intended to try. To her delight he nodded his head, questioned her more, and voiced a desire to see how following the Lord would help him.

Ina suggested that it would be a good idea if he could live for a while with a Christian family, so long as he was willing to be taught and disciplined by them. He agreed. Ina had thought of us, and Rudolph came to stay.

He quickly struck up a warm friendship with my mother, sharing her love for good pictures and books and antique furniture, and they spent many hours talking together in her flat. We were sorry when Rudolph decided it was time for him to move back to London; "dry" and saying he would be alright now that he had discovered a relationship with God.

There were others, during the conference season, who came just for a day, and were healed. Like Kitty.

Kitty had been in mental hospital on and off for seventeen years, and had been allowed out of hospital for the day in order to come to the meeting with her friends, John and Pam Pond. Jean prayed with her and as she did so she sensed that the Holy Spirit was healing Kitty deep down. The first time I saw Kitty, she was sitting in the kitchen drinking tea. A woman in her late thirties, dark-haired, of medium height, she barely acknowledged my greeting. I noticed how tightly she clasped her mug of tea, drinking with quick, nervous gulps. Jean and Pam Pond were with her.

"Fom now on, Kitty," I heard Jean say to her, "you're going to get better ..."

Pam Pond rang the next week to say that Kitty was out of hospital and staying with them.

"I'm amazed at her progress, Faith," she said.

Even so, Pam was often on the phone asking, "What do I do?" Kitty was still far from stable; she too needed loving into complete wholeness.

In the summer of 1969 we ran our second camp programme and many of the same people came again to help. I was openly sharing now the vision the Lord had given me of a city of refuge. Denis Ball, an Elim minister from Bournemouth, told us what the Lord had shown him and his wife, Pinky, many years before.

Denis and Pinky had been coming out to the meetings since they first started. I always knew when Denis was around because of his infectious deep-throated laugh, which reverberated all over the house, and if it wasn't his laugh then it was Denis singing as he washed up dishes at the kitchen sink. Somehow Denis's rich baritone leading in song spills over into all my memories of that summer.

Denis and Pinky had moved to Bournemouth from Bedford some years previously with a strong sense that God was calling them to the area for a specific purpose. They had been members of an old Catholic Apostolic church in Bedford. During a time of prayer and fasting, Denis had received a vision: he saw a large oak tree, apparently dead. The tree was suddenly cut without any weapon. It was not completely severed, and out of the wounded trunk appeared a tiny shoot which became a new tree growing out of the old. This new tree gave life to the old, but at the same time it received life from it.

Denis, usually sceptical of "visions and the like" was nevertheless convinced that this one was from God. It represented what God was going to do in the Church, that "out of the old was coming the new", each giving life to the other. He believed that the vision was in some way bound up with their move to Bournemouth.

Their first years in Bournemouth were difficult ones; things did not go well at the church where Denis was co-pastor. They moved to another church, and yet it seemed to Denis and Pinky that the work they had been called to share was not going to be established in a church building at all. Increasingly Denis could visualise what God had in store for them.

"I could see a recording studio. I could see missionaries coming in and resting and being revived. I could see ministers and clergy coming for conferences and sessions. I could see camps. It was a centre, a complex, caring for people, ministering to folk with needs. I could see, as part of it all, music and drama and the arts being restored to their rightful place in the Church and being used also in a therapeutic capacity. I could see crafts and even several small industries. More than this I could see the life which was pulsating through the whole, entering into people as they came and went. I could see us going out into various parts of Britain. I could see us abroad ..." Denis told us excitedly later.

"How is it going to happen and where?" Denis and Pinky wondered. Sometimes they got into their car and drove around looking at various large properties. Perhaps God wanted them to buy a large house and establish such a complex, but they never felt convinced that this was what they should do.

"When I met you both I suddenly felt 'This is it'," Denis now told Tom and me.

Well, I thought, if the Lord is going to do even half of these things he'll have to send us some more help: and not just part-time help either. Certainly I could do with someone around to help me with the cooking and the housework, with writing letters and planning meetings: someone who could pray with people and encourage them, someone living with us and available full-time.

Earlier in the year, two young people, Valerie Lester and Tony Churchill, had approached Elmer with a question.

"Why don't you start a Bible college here?" they asked.

They knew that Elmer had run a Bible school in Australia and had founded a Christian high school in Hong Kong. Why shouldn't he use his gifts in the same way in England?

Elmer had been waiting for some such indication of what the Lord might be wanting him to do next.

"If there are six young people like you interested, I'll do it," he told them, after thinking the matter over.

Now with the autumn approaching twelve students had signed up for Christian Life College, as Elmer had named it. More were expected. The students would do an ordinary job during the day and would attend classes in the evenings. Classes would be held at the Manor School, and Elmer had asked Tom and Denis to be on the teaching faculty. Rex Meakin, a retired Anglican minister from Loughborough who with his wife Betty was moving into the area, had also agreed to be a tutor.

The Post Green ministry was growing steadily. I felt still more strongly how much I needed a helper.

"But, how do you know when you have a prophecy?" Tom's niece, Sheila, Jane's elder daughter, wanted to know.

Whenever Ina Northey was staying with us the children gathered round her. She had a lot to say that interested them – her story remarkably like that of the prodigal son in the Bible. Like Rudolph, she had been a heavy drinker. She came from a wealthy family, but soon used up all her money, and ended tending pigs on a pig farm. By arrangement, the farmer paid her in drink, not cash. Since she had no money for food she ate the refuse she fed to the pigs.

This was but one remarkable episode in her life and it was during this period that she came to know God and was freed of alcoholism. In time she was ordained as a deaconess and had gone to live among the Canadian Indians in British Columbia.

Ina was also the kind of person who could explain spiritual matters in ways that were simple and easy to understand. She answered Sheila's question in her usual clear and matter of fact fashion.

"Well," she said, "it's all tied up with loving people and being concerned for them. And prayer. Prayer and prophecy are very closely linked; some prayers are prophecies, it's just a matter of whether one has the faith to speak them out as such. For instance, say I'm praying for Faith like this." She laid her hand on my shoulder, and began praying for me, then once underway she started to prophesy.

I only had half an ear for what Ina was saying. After all, it was only a demonstration for the children, and much of what I heard her say I had heard before: how the Lord was going to use me, the ways in which he desired to bless us and so on. But then I heard something different.

"I'm going to send someone to help you ...", she was saying.

I pricked up my ears. That I was interested in.

I began to look around for the person God was going to send, expecting to meet her (obviously, I thought, it had to be a her) any moment. But as summer turned again to autumn and we entered our third conference season, I almost forgot Ina's prophecy.

That autumn Tom was asked by Michael Harper if he would become a trustee of the Fountain Trust. We already knew many of those who were closely associated with Michael

and Jeanne in supporting the work of the Trust, among them
Reg and Lucia East and David and Daphne Mills. David was
now working full-time for the Fountain Trust. We discovered
they were talking about the need for a centre run by a resident
community of Spirit-filled people. They were already looking
for a house that might be used for that purpose.

We went one weekend to attend a gathering of the Fountain
Trust staff and trustees, and for the first time we met David
and Jill Ford. David was a doctor working in London and he,
like Tom, had just become a trustee.

"And where do you come from?" David asked us politely.

We told him that our home, Post Green, was near to Poole
in Dorset. We doubted that he had heard of Lytchett Minster.

Neither he nor Jill was listening. Both of them were staring
strangely at us.

Like the others they were wondering whether God wanted
them to sell up and become part of a Spirit-filled community.
While she had been praying about this Jill clearly heard the
Lord say to her, "The pattern is Post Green." At least, those
were the words that came, but they made no sense. Could it
have been the Lord? She told David and together they asked
the Lord for some confirmation.

Later that day David felt impressed to turn to Isaiah 57
and to read that chapter. There was nothing in the content of
the chapter that spoke to him, but there tucked into verse 5
he found the word *green* and three verses later there stood out
the word *post*. What to make of this they didn't know, but
having asked for some confirmation they could hardly ignore
it totally. If it was God, they concluded, it would make sense
in time.

No wonder they now stood transfixed staring at us.

experienced than she in caring for people and praying for the
sick, constantly found myself over-anxious about those we
ministered to.

"Faith," Jean often had occasion to remind me, "we prayed,
now leave it at that. It's in the Lord's hands."

But the fact that she had taught herself to do this did not
mean that she cared less than I did – I knew that.

"Compassion" – that was the word I wanted. I never
ceased to be moved by Jean's penetrating but gentle sensitivity
to people in need; it seemed to give wings to her faith, and
yet she never prayed for people out of sentiment, always
waited for the leading of the Holy Spirit. I did not find it
hard to understand why Jean had such a remarkable ministry
to the sick.

"Is Mrs. Darnall in?" someone would ask, standing on the
doorstep at Post Green. Or, "I just wanted to have a word with
Jean Darnall," a voice would say over the telephone. Jean and
Elmer had moved to Rest Harrow by then, but few people
had their address. Most often Jean would be away from home
anyway. I would tell her when she came back who had called
or rung.

"You need to pray with them yourself," she would tell me.

"But they're wanting you."

"It's God who heals."

I knew she was right. Sometimes I grinned ruefully,
remembering how in the past it had been Tom's mother people
had wanted to see, not me. Now it was someone else. I had
learnt then not to feel swamped, to appreciate I had my own
gifts. Now I knew God wanted me to pray for those who
came seeking help, which meant that I needed to learn all Jean
could teach me. Travelling around the States with her was an
excellent opportunity.

We returned to England accompanied by two rebellious
teenagers whom I had invited to visit us. As a result our family
holiday in Scourie that summer was somewhat less peaceful
than usual. However, the two young men mellowed while with
us and discovered a new faith in God, so it was worth it.

12

So It Is With the Body

JEAN AND I sat drinking coffee in a cafe in Portland, Oregon. We were taking a break before a meeting we were scheduled to speak at later that afternoon. Jean had invited me to accompany her on a short visit to the States. Now that she and Elmer had decided to stay in England, Jean was spending a month visiting friends who had supported her financially and with their prayers since she had been in Europe. We had visited several cities on the Western seaboard, sharing what God was doing in England and at Post Green.

Jean looked up from the letter she had been reading from LaDonna. Some movement in the street outside had caught her attention. I saw a look of deep concern cross her face. Outside, a woman was being helped from a car into a wheelchair. Disabled, she needed two men to lift her; an exercise that was obviously painful for her. I looked at Jean again. Concern was the wrong word.

Jean sensed my watching her and smiled.

"I guess part of me always feels for someone in pain, Faith," she said.

I had learnt a lot about Jean since the day she had first come to lunch at Post Green. She and Elmer, Tom and I came from very different backgrounds and we had our disagreements – some of them strongly expressed – but we were all four learning to appreciate one another. We had worked together closely for over a year now. Tom and I had helped them to understand and to adapt to English ways; Jean and Elmer had given us good advice about the ministry that was developing at Post Green. I was glad for such a friend as Jean. I, less

Not long after our return from Scourie, Jean rang from a conference centre in Devon to ask if we would consider having a young woman to stay.

"It would be good for her to be part of a family for a while," she said.

So Carol came to live with us, a withdrawn and sullen girl. Then Bridget telephoned from school.

' Mum, there's a new girl I'm sharing a room with and she's terribly worried about her mother who's having a nervous breakdown or something like that. I've talked to her about Jesus and how he can heal her mother. I hope it's alright."

Bridget sounded anxious: had she done the right thing? and please would I go and see her friend's mother and pray with her?

I drove to Salisbury to meet Anne, who was staying in a hotel there. Her husband had a governmental post abroad and Anne was in England visiting her children, hence the hotel. She took me to her room and as I went in I stumbled over a pile of clothes. Littering the floor were books and magazines and more discarded clothes. In order not to tread on them, I stooped to pick some up.

"I'm sorry," she said, "you see I can't do that. At least, sometimes at night I can manage to tidy up a bit, but in the daytime I ... well ... I just can't."

"That's alright," I said, "I'm not a very tidy person either."

I could see that she must be an attractive woman when she was well. Now she was pale and drawn. She made an attempt to smile and be polite, but it was a tremendous effort for her.

I told her I understood all about fears and the havoc that they can play with one; how Jesus had set me free and how I had seen him set others free. She listened, but I could see she was at a loss to know how to reply. In the end, I prayed with her and suggested that we might meet again some other time.

As I prayed, I had the strong conviction that she would feel better in three days. So certain was I, that I told her so. I was not surprised that she looked doubtful, but I left her with that reassurance.

Three days later she rang to say that she did indeed feel much better.

"In fact," she said, "I feel quite different. I'd like to come and talk with you some more if I may."

"I'd like that," I told her.

Soon Jean was asking if we could have a second person to stay. Kitty, who had visited us earlier in the year, had left the Ponds and moved to London. She wanted to see if she could manage on her own. But she was not doing too well. Jean had met and talked with her again at a church in London.

"I don't think she'd be a lot of bother," she said to us, "but I believe she needs the kind of love you can give her. And I believe she's a person the Lord wants to use."

Then Rudolph had been on the phone.

"I want to come home," he said.

Rudolph hadn't been doing too well managing on his own either. We had advised him to attach himself to a church where he could continue to find the same kind of encouragement and support that we had given him. But he had not done so. Now he was back on the bottle again.

Our family was growing rapidly.

We called a family council. Tom and I had agreed with the children that we would not take any decisions that affected our home without first consulting them. We were impressed on these occasions by the mature way that all four handled these conversations; their apposite questioning of Tom and me, their sensitivity to what the Lord was saying and doing, their willingness to support us in what we felt was right.

"But Mum, we don't want you tiring yourself out." It would usually be Lizzie who voiced this, but she spoke for all of them.

At boarding school nearby, Bridget and Lizzie came home most weekends and so had close contact with those who came to stay. Christopher, still at Eton, was home less often. Sarah had left school and was at Hull University taking a degree course in English and theology. What God had done for Sarah had been attested by her final school report.

"Civilised person!" she had exclaimed in mock horror as we read it with her.

"We shall miss the judgement and helpfulness of a mature and civilised person," her head teacher had written. We had turned to the headmistress's report and read, "Sarah has shown a new poise without and a new tranquility within, and has been more whole-heartedly ready and responsible than in any previous term. This has been a fine and rewarding conclusion."

Like her head teacher, I too had come to appreciate Sarah's judgement and helpfulness. She had a remarkable insight into the needs of those who came to visit, and a quick and deep appreciation of what God wanted to do in their lives.

With the prospect of having more people in the home, I was glad that I also had met the person God had promised to send to help.

Jeanne Hinton had been working with the Fountain Trust and Tom and I first met her at one of their staff gatherings. Jeanne came to spend a week's holiday with us; and the same week Anne, whom I had visited in the hotel in Salisbury, came to stay. Jeanne, who was experienced at talking and praying with people and who knew her Bible a lot better than I did, was able to encourage Anne and to support me in counselling her. As a result, Anne, who had confessed herself an agnostic, was saying that she had recovered a former belief in God. Jeanne had joined me on a speaking engagement, giving her testimony of how she had been filled with the Spirit whilst working as a full-time youth leader at a church in South London.

For the first time, I felt really supported in what I was doing.

"That's the person I'm going to send to help you."

I had long since stopped sizing people up in the hope that they might be the one. As this thought about Jeanne flashed through my mind I was startled. It could hardly be Jeanne, she was firmly committed elsewhere.

Unknown to us, however, Jeanne, who had joined the staff of the Fountain Trust a year previously, had at that time said

to Michael, "I think it will be only for a year. I have a feeling
something else is going to open up that the Lord wants me to
do." Now the year was already at an end and Jeanne had begun
to wonder whether she had been right. Not long after her
visit to us she became convinced that God wanted her to join
us at Post Green.

So Jeanne came to live with us, along with Carol and Rudolph. And Kitty. Kitty it was decided would not live at Post
Green, but with "Dunks" (Miss Dunkley, my mother-in-
law's friend) in the house next to Jane's.

This arrangement was not very satisfactory. Kitty was
restless at night; constantly in and out of the kitchen making
herself cups of tea. She had a job working in the canteen at a
nearby army establishment. It was not a very demanding job,
but demanding enough for Kitty who had not been able to
keep any job for long. She was still fearful of any kind of
responsibility and needed constant reassurance that she could
cope. She would call on Jane, or be in and out of Post Green
seeking support.

"It's really too much of a strain on Dunks," Jane told me.

Kitty would have preferred to have been at Post Green, like
Carol and Rudolph. In the end we agreed to this: on certain
conditions.

I realised that she needed to establish new patterns of self
discipline. "If you do come," I told her, "you'll have to keep
to a definite schedule. And one thing is essential: that you
have a regular time of prayer and Bible reading each day."
We established that the best time for her to do this was when
she came home from work.

God had given me an especial love for Kitty. When she was
not worrying about herself she was the kind of person who
brought a lot of life into the house. Her singing and laughter
were in contrast to Carol, who most often was moody and
difficult. I loved Carol too, but Kitty in the right mood would
often be the one to cheer me up if I felt harassed or worried.
At one time she had been a Methodist lay preacher and she
loved to share with me what she had been reading and thinking

about in her prayer times. Often it was very near to what I had been thinking myself.

"What a strength she'll be to us all when she's really stabilised," I said to Jeanne and Tom. They agreed. We all enjoyed having her around.

The first day Kitty came back from work, after she had moved into Post Green, I was busy cooking. David and Daphne Mills and their three children had come to stay, so we were quite a number for supper. David and Daphne were coming to join us in the autumn; David to teach at the Bible college and both of them to support us in the work.

"Do you think you could spend some time with Kitty and see she has her prayer time?" I asked Jeanne. "Maybe it would be good if for a while you did a Bible study with her daily."

I had caught Jeanne unprepared.

"What shall I do?" she wanted to know.

"Just share what you've been reading yourself," I said, and shooed them both out of the kitchen and got on with the supper.

Thirty minutes later there was an anxious call from upstairs. "I think you'd better come, Faith."

I was just about to ring the gong for supper, but Jeanne was leaning over the banisters, beckoning me.

I hesitated; I didn't want to get involved in anything right before supper.

"I'm afraid you'll have to," Jeanne's voice was urgent now.

Upstairs in Jeanne's room I found Kitty writhing on the floor in an epileptic fit.

"She was alright," said Jeanne apologetically, "to begin with anyway. She started to get upset and angry when I shared with her what I had been studying. I tried to calm her. But, as you can see," she finished lamely, "it didn't work."

"Go and get Tom," I said, "and perhaps you can see that supper gets under way."

Tom carried Kitty into her room. She had recovered now, but instead was beginning to sob hysterically. I stayed and talked to her. Something Jeanne had said had made her angry, but she would not talk about it. Since she refused to talk I told her to get up and come downstairs. But this she also refused to do. I decided to leave her.

"What on earth did you say to her?" I asked Jeanne. Supper was over, but Jeanne and David and Daphne sat with me while I ate mine. Tom had a church council meeting and had left.

"I read that passage from Hebrews chapter 3 where the writer warns the people not to harden their hearts as the people of Israel hardened their hearts and rebelled against God in the wilderness," Jeanne told us.

"I was sharing with Kitty my thoughts about the Israelites. In Egypt they sighed and groaned because of their bondage and cried to God to deliver them. He did so. But later in the wilderness they complained that it would have been better for them to have died in Egypt. Because they were having such a hard time in the wilderness they began to think that they had been better off in Egypt – forgetting that they had been in bondage, and forgetting too God's promise to bring them into a land of plenty.

"You know," said Jeanne, warming to her theme now, "I was thinking how much easier it is for God to take us out of a bad experience, than it is for him to take us into a good one. Both need our co-operation, but usually we are quicker to accept God's help for the former than we are for the latter. Strange isn't it?"

Remembering why she was telling us, Jeanne stopped. "I really wasn't preaching at Kitty," she said, "I was only sharing with her what I had heard God say to me. Shall I go up and try to talk some more with her?"

"No," I said, "leave her alone."

Daphne looked worried. "I think you're being very hard on Kitty, Faith," she said. "Let me go."

"O.K. you go," I agreed.

By the time Daphne came downstairs again, Tom had returned from his meeting and had joined us in the drawing room. Rudolph was up talking with my mother, and Carol was over at Jane's.

"Kitty's getting up. She'll come down and join us for a while before we go to bed," Daphne told us.

When Kitty came down she was relaxed and cheerful again and apologised for the earlier disturbance. The evening might have ended without further ado, if I had not felt compelled to question Kitty further.

The moment I did so, she was angry again. Her face clouded.

"You're all against me," she accused us. "Why don't you leave me alone. I was perfectly alright." She was shouting now, directing her anger at me. "If only you'd leave me alone ..."

"You're not alright, Kitty ..." David moved across to sit beside her. His voice was gentle, soothing her. "God's put his finger on something important, hasn't he?"

But Kitty had withdrawn into herself, her face hard and forbidding. She wouldn't say any more. David continued to talk, trying to draw her out, but with little result. At only one point did he get any real response. "When you can believe ..." he began. "I can't ... I can't believe ..." The words came out before Kitty realised she had spoken. She quickly shut up again.

Now an hour later we sat silent. Kitty had not moved. None of us had anything more to say.

"Who is it Kitty that you haven't forgiven?" Tom asked. He always seemed to have this way of cutting right into a conversation with a thought that seemed totally irrelevant. I opened my mouth to suggest we all went to bed rather than prolong the conversation any further. But Tom had already opened his Bible and had begun to read.

"Beware then of your own hearts, dear brothers, in case you should find that they, too, are evil and unbelieving and are leading you away from the living God ... Today, if you hear God's voice speaking to you, do not harden your hearts against him, as the people of Israel did when they rebelled against him in the desert."

We all sat up, suddenly attentive. Tom was reading the

same passage that Jeanne had read to Kitty earlier. Yet Tom
had not been there when Jeanne had told us about this.

He went on, "And who were those people I spoke of, who
heard God's voice speaking to them but then rebelled against
him? They were the ones who came out of Egypt with Moses
their leader. And who was it who made God angry for all
those forty years? These same people who sinned and as a
result died in the wilderness . . . And why couldn't they go on?
Because they didn't trust him."

Tom closed his Bible and looked at Kitty.

"You know why you can't trust God, Kitty?" he said. "It's
because at some point you've hardened your heart and not
done as he said."

Tom got up from his chair and went to kneel beside her.
Quietly he took her hand. "It has to do with your mother hasn't
it? You haven't been able to forgive your mother for something
she did."

While he had been talking Kitty had shown for the first
time since the conversation started that she was really listening. Tears sprang to her eyes as he began to talk about a hard
heart; now as he spoke of her mother great sobs shook her
body.

She talked then and told us things that she had never confessed to anyone before. Afterwards she prayed and asked
the Lord for his forgiveness, and we prayed and asked him to
cleanse and heal her.

We all sat back and looked at our watches. It was 2 a.m.
Rudolph and Carol must have gone to bed long ago.

Later I lay in bed and thought not only about Kitty, but
about Jeanne and David and Daphne and Tom and myself.
Each of us had played a significant part in what had happened.
It had not been anything we had worked out beforehand. We
had each slotted in at the right time with the right word, but it
had been in such a natural, matter of fact, way: just doing or
saying the next thing that came into mind. We had followed
on from one another; one had picked up where the other had
left off. If any of us had not done or said what we felt to be

right then the evening would most probably have ended up a disaster instead of a triumph.

There was a scripture somewhere, I thought, that fitted this. The next morning I picked up Tom's Bible which was still lying on the sofa in the drawing room, and thumbing through the epistles I found what I was looking for in chapter 12 of 1 Corinthians:

"Now God gives us many kinds of special abilities, but it is the same Holy Spirit who is the source of them all. There are different kinds of service to God, but it is the same Lord we are serving. There are many ways in which God works in our lives, but it is the same God who does the work in and through all of us, who are his. The Holy Spirit displays God's power through each of us as a means of helping the entire church."

I skipped a few verses and picked up the passage again at verse 12. "Our bodies have many parts, but the many parts make up only one body when they are all put together. So it is with the 'body' of Christ . . ."

"So it is with the 'body' of Christ . . .", those words went round and round in my mind the rest of the day. What we had experienced together that evening was God's plan and purpose for all Christians. For the Church. For us at Post Green. I had not seen it so clearly before – the importance of the body; not just so many individuals at work, but one body.

Kitty came home that afternoon looking quite a different person.

"Do you know, Faith, I think the Lord has healed me of my epilepsy," she told me.

I questioned her further.

While we had been praying the night before she had had a definite assurance that this was so.

"Should I throw away my pills?" was her next question.

Kitty had pills that she took three times a day to control her epilepsy.

"How do you feel about it," I asked, "inside there?" I

poked her tummy. "It's a matter of where your faith really is. How do you *feel*?"

"Well, I don't know ..." she said.

"Then let's leave it for the moment," I concluded.

Three weeks later Kitty threw her pills away: she knew it was the right time for her to do so.

Letters came from all over the country: seeking advice, asking us to pray for this or that person. A good many were addressed to Jean, but she had not the time to answer them all. I offered to help her out, and as a result I found myself writing – saying the same things over and over again. Repeatedly I wrote that divine healing is not mind over matter – its basis is trust in God's word; I shared how to receive and act on the word that God speaks; how to withstand the devil's attempts to undermine faith; the importance of being in a right relationship with others as well as with God; the danger of any entanglement with the occult. We said the same to people who came forward for prayer at the meetings and camps.

"Wouldn't it be a good idea if we could get all these ideas together and were able to produce them in leaflet form," I said to Jeanne. "Then I could enclose the appropriate leaflet with a letter and not have to repeat myself continually."

She nodded.

"Do you think you could do it?" I asked.

Jeanne had been a journalist for a while some years back and still did some writing at times.

"Yes, I think so," she said, "but it won't be easy condensing what you usually say into leaflets. I guess we'd need to put some time aside to work on it together."

Getting time to work together on such a project was not easy. We would sit down to prepare a Bible study or talk over some plans and inevitably that would be the signal for someone to turn up with a problem, or for the telephone to ring, or something to boil over on the cooker.

"I think if Jeanne and I could get away quietly for a day we might do better," I said to Tom. "Brownsea Island would be a good place."

Brownsea Island is the largest island in Poole harbour. A fifteen minute boat ride from Poole Quay, part of it is a bird sanctuary. Quiet and peaceful with an unusually relaxed atmosphere, it is the home of many exotically plumed peacocks.

"Tuesday would be a good day," I added.

"Have you forgotten that that's the day Pastor Wurmbrand is speaking in Bournemouth?" he reminded me.

"Yes, but that's in the evening," I replied. "We'll be back well before then."

"What do you mean by 'being founded on truth'?" Jeanne pressed me. Often I had difficulty communicating with her when we got down to talking things over. I had the same problem with others. I was never satisfied that they had fully grasped what I wanted them to understand. It was essential now that Jeanne did understand if we were to write these leaflets together.

I explained what I meant.

"There was a time when I was stupidly anxious if any of the family were late home. In my mind I saw them lying by the side of the road, badly injured or dead. My thoughts were deceiving me, but I had a hard time not believing them. Then I realised there was a connection between this fear and a car accident I had been in.

"I had been driving Christopher and another child home from school when I was blinded by the sun and ran into the back of a stationary lorry. The children were concussed and I had a broken rib. We were taken to hospital in an ambulance, but the worst thing was having to ring the other child's mother to tell her what had happened. It was a little while after this accident that I began to be fearful about the family.

When I saw this was the cause, I was able to control my fear. But I needed God's help to enable me to do so.

"You see, the devil is quick to take advantage of such situations. He is the father of lies and he seeks every opportunity to sow them in our minds; to get us into bondage to himself. But Jesus is the truth and his word is truth. If we are secure in him we are safe from the attacks of the enemy. This means not only believing the truth; it means living it too. It means building one's life on "those things that are true". Like St. Paul says in Philippians, "Whatever is true, whatever is honourable, whatever is just, whatever is pure, whatever is lovely, whatever is gracious ... think about these things.""

"I think I understand what you mean now," Jeanne said at last. "And anyway," she added, rolling over on the grass and throwing a bit of sandwich at a peacock that had been pestering us all day, "I've just thought of a good title for our first leaflet. We'll call it 'It's a Lie'."

It was to be the first of several such leaflets we worked on together and which we were to use increasingly in correspondence and counselling. But we had misjudged our timing. When we arrived at the harbour the last ferry to the mainland had gone. It was fortunate that I knew a member of the island staff, and was able to consult him. There was another private boat leaving in an hour, he said. He could arrange for us to cross to the mainland on that. I rang home.

"But, what about supper?" Tom sounded extremely grumpy on the other end of the telephone.

I remembered that I had bought some steak earlier that day and that it was still in the back of the car parked over at Poole Quay.

"Do you think you could find something else?" I suggested. There's food in the fridge."

Luckily, Tom enjoyed cooking. I doubted, however, that he was going to enjoy it this time. He didn't sound in the mood.

We didn't miss the meeting in Bournemouth, and Tom said little on our return. But I knew he was upset with us. I wished it wasn't always such a trauma when Jeanne and I wanted to do something together.

It was to be quite a while before Tom told me his side of the story. Over the months since Jeanne, Kitty, Carol and Rudolph had come to live with us he had kept quiet about the way he was feeling. Almost too quiet. Did he agree we were doing the right thing? I asked him on occasions. "Yes," he said, and I took his word for it.

But we saw a lot less of each other. He was out much of the time, busier than ever. I had given up my work as hospital librarian and was no longer a J.P. If Tom had had fewer outside commitments it would have been easier for him. Life at Post Green was rarely peaceful; driving home from a full day of engagements, he never knew what kind of evening lay ahead and some days dreaded returning for this reason. Unknown to me, he was finding the close relationship between Jeanne and myself hard to accept. He was beginning to feel excluded.

While we had been relaxing on Brownsea, writing a leaflet on how to deal with fears and anxieties, Tom had decided he had had enough. He had started to rationalise his thoughts and feelings, and had convinced himself that he was a hindrance – to me and to the things that I felt to be so important. It would be far better, he decided, if he was not around. On a sudden impulse, he packed a suitcase and prepared to leave.

Coming downstairs he met Vic Ramsey who was staying with us at the time. Vic sensed Tom's unease and asked him what was wrong. If Vic had not been there, Tom might have walked out of the house and I would certainly have known then that he was far from happy.

But Tom never failed to do what he knew to be right. He was there with us listening to Pastor Wurmbrand that evening. Jeanne had no idea either that Tom felt the way he did: they got on well together.

"What do you think about Carol getting a flat in Bournemouth?" I asked Tom. It was some months later. Carol had blossomed during this time; she was an extremely intelligent and able young woman, attractive now that she was no longer withdrawn and sullen. She was talking of getting a job in Bournemouth and living there. She wanted to be near enough to stay in close contact with us. Rudolph too was talking of getting a bed-sitter in Bournemouth and keeping in touch in the same way.

"I think it's a good idea," said Tom. "I don't know that I've ever been too happy about our having needy people in the house for a prolonged period of time."

Kitty had moved out of the house into a caravan in the paddock; she preferred this. It gave her more privacy, she said. Now she planned to move into a home of her own in the village.

It looked as though our family was going to be dispersed. How would Kitty and Carol and Rudolph make out?

One thing I knew; that God wanted Tom and Jeanne and me to be as one. Our unity was essential for the continuation of the work that God was wanting to do at Post Green.

13

How Can I Face Failure?

I LOOKED AROUND at my audience and grasped my notes firmly.

"I was a person who used to find loving totally impossible. My mother will bear me out in this. I used to hold her and everyone else at arm's length. I didn't like to be close to anyone at all.

"After we became filled with the Spirit, Tom would say, 'How easy it is to love!' But I would retort, 'It's not easy; it's not a bit easy'."

As well as our weekend conferences, we had begun to run Thursday night teach-ins. I was speaking at one of these teach-ins on the subject of "Our love in Christ".

Meetings were no longer held in the house. Two hundred were as many as we could cram in and most weekends we had four to five hundred coming. The house had deteriorated from constantly moving carpets and furniture about, and the staircase was in danger of imminent collapse from having so many people sitting on it.

We now had a Spandrel Dome, a large tent made of terylene erected on a geodetic frame, which stood in the paddock, and meetings were held in this tent, or "the dome" as we called it.

"My experience goes along with the way St. Paul taught the Corinthians," I continued. "He told them 'to pursue love ...' I believe that to love people as Jesus loves them is something we have to search after. We have to make it our aim. It's jolly hard work and often it hurts too. 'Put on love,' Paul said to the Colossians. It's not an entirely spontaneous action."

"Tom's mother taught me a lot about loving people. Those of you who knew her will know what I mean when I say that. It was from her that I first learnt the need to be openly affectionate with people; that there is a healing in the way we greet each other – in the way we look at and even touch each other. And I've come to realise this even more latterly as we've experienced God's love being poured out among us in such a powerful way.

"Nowadays I do find it easier to love people and to love a lot of people. I believe that we need to take the initial steps in seeking to love, all the time trusting that God is going to be helping us. Edgar Trout taught me to pray, 'Give me more of the love of Jesus,' and I did this for some time. But I was quite frightened when I realised that I was beginning to get this love. Because there's power in the love of Jesus.

"Sometimes God gives me a special love for a person, and usually it's for their healing. But more and more I am learning how costly it is to love people this way. It has opened me up to a lot of criticism and misunderstanding even from those closest to me. Some say 'You put too much of yourself into it, Faith,' or 'It's not the love of Jesus; it's you, Faith.' And indeed it is difficult to know the difference. Such comments hurt, and I've gone back to the Lord time and again with the question, 'How can I love people and not *feel* anything? How can one love without actually loving?' And I hear him reassuring me 'You can't'."

Preparing this talk I had thought back to a conversation Jeanne and I had the first summer she was with us.

"I don't know what to think," she had said. "At times I'm just plain scared."

She was referring to the love that she felt for me and I for her. I could accept that this was a love that God had given us for each other, and that he had a special purpose in it. Often I joked that it was necessary for God to give us this love, otherwise we would never have got on together. Like me, Jeanne had very much a mind and a will of her own. But now she felt trapped by our love

"There's no other word for it than that, Faith," she complained. "I don't feel free any longer."

I thought I knew what God was doing. Earlier in the year Jeanne had needed to make a major decision. She had not long before started to write a book about her experiences in youth work and was under contract to have it completed by the end of the year. She had thought at first that she could manage to do this and help me in the house – going back to her flat in London for just a few weeks at a time to do further research. But it was difficult to be part of what God was doing at Post Green and have a major commitment elsewhere. What should she do? What was to be the priority in her life? What did God want?

She had prayed about this and in answer God had said nothing about the book she was writing, but he spoke to her of love.

"Many think that life is so short that they dare not give themselves unrestrainedly in love. We have been reborn for eternity, and love is one of the few things we can carry with us," she read in her daily Bible reading notes, and the words stuck.

She decided then and there that God wanted her at Post Green.

"I know that God wants me here," she told me. "And part of the reason is to help me discover what it means to love people the way God loves them."

I hurt when Jeanne told me that – both because I was glad, but also because I knew so well the pain entailed as well as the joy. She was not finding it easy.

Sitting sunning ourselves in the orchard early that summer, we had talked more about the matter.

"I believe one reason God's given you this love for me is to keep you here," I told her. "You're important to what God is doing among us, and yet you can't see exactly what he is doing. You're the kind of person who always wants to understand what's happening. I think if only you could bring yourself to say yes to our relationship, to loving me and to being here – and stopped questioning everything – then you wouldn't feel so trapped."

Jeanne was dubious and we talked late into the afternoon. Finally she said, "Well, maybe it's God, maybe it's not, but I can see I need to make up my mind. For the moment I'm going to believe it is ... everything seems to point that way."

She had stuck to her resolution too. It had made life a good deal easier for both of us.

Speaking at the teach-in in the dome, I continued to share what we were learning – all of us – about loving people.

"God's love is strong and enduring, and he always wants the best for us – to bring us into harmony with himself, because that is where we find peace and joy and love. But often this means his saying some hard things to us. Those who met Jesus felt the quality of his love and this enabled them to receive correction from him too.

"Our love has to be of the same quality: an unwavering love. Not a 'here today and gone tomorrow' affair, but deep, strong and relentless. The kind of love that enables people to accept the truth from us, and helps them to change. Knowing they are loved they drop their shields, let go of long-standing hurts and resentments and are willing to see themselves and to be seen as they really are – both the good and the bad.

"The woman at the well of Samaria and the woman taken in adultery knew that Jesus forgave them even before he spoke to them of their sin. It was the same experience Peter had after he denied Jesus. It was what caused him to weep rather than to curse. Such love transforms people and their situations.

"This is what it means to love people with God's love ..."

Teaching is not my strong point; it is more Jeanne's gift. However, having to teach from time to time had enabled me to collect my thoughts together and to understand more clearly how things worked, or ought to work.

I understood that it is this love that reaches into people and helps them to uncover all the hurt and bruised bits of themselves and to expose them to the light of God's forgiveness and healing. I knew too that this is not all that has to happen; more has to follow if a person is to be complete. Love enables us to change, but even so we are presented with a choice – whether to press on to the point where we become mature in Christ.

We saw this working in people differently. Some like Anne, the mother of Bridget's schoolfriend, were determined to press on.

Anne needed this determination for she had experienced some major setbacks since visiting us. Having re-joined her husband overseas, her fears came back with even greater force. She sent letter-tapes telling of her growing despair that she would ever be well again. I sent back long letters encouraging her. Part of Anne's difficulty was her inability to carry any action through. Even putting on a gramophone record was too much for her. Luckily she had servants to run the house. But, there had been one hopeful sign: she managed bit by bit to struggle through Catharine Marshall's *Beyond Our Selves*, a book I had lent her. This helped to build up her faith in God. But Jesus remained a vague historical figure: whether she believed in him as the Son of God she didn't know.

As Christmas 1970 drew near and her daughters were due to join them for the holidays, Anne put herself voluntarily into hospital rather than face them. More and more one thought began to dominate: if she could get to Post Green she would be healed.

On Boxing Day 1971 she boarded a Boeing 707 and flew back to England. She rang from London Airport to say she had arrived but we knew nothing of her plans and were away skiing in Switzerland. Jeanne answered the phone. We would be back in five days, she told her. But so desperate did Anne sound that Jeanne cabled us in Switzerland to tell us of the situation.

Even when we returned home to Post Green it was not a convenient time to have Anne to stay. It coincided with the weekend we were erecting the dome and a large party of helpers had been organised. We had arranged a sewing and upholstery party in the house: making new curtains and repairing chairs whose innards had long since escaped from worn and frayed covering.

"You can come," I told an anxious sounding Anne in the end, "but I'm afraid I won't have much time to talk until after the weekend."

Carol, too, had asked if she could stay the weekend. She had broken her arm at work and was in plaster. She would not be able to help with the sewing and I was uncertain how she would cope with our being so occupied, while she sat idle. She could still be demanding in such a circumstance.

When Anne arrived she saw immediately that I had not been exaggerating: it was not the best time for her to visit. But having made it to Post Green she was not easily to be daunted. She was certain that God had told her to come, and as she prayed about the situation she seemed to hear him say that Carol would be the one to help her.

"I believe God's going to use you to show me something important," she told Carol.

Carol, as I feared, was already slopping around the house, looking bored and unhappy. It seemed unlikely that she would be of any encouragement to Anne. I was wrong. Carol, who had a real insight into the truth of God's word and a love for her Bible, was the one who sat with Anne reading to her and answering her questions.

Over that weekend Anne experienced God's presence in an entirely fresh way. At the end she said that she knew without doubt that Jesus is the Son of God and that she herself had been taken from the kingdom of darkness and had entered his kingdom – the kingdom of light. Anne knew exactly what is meant by the Bible terminology of kingdoms of darkness and light: she had lived in darkness for long enough.

It is not easy to live in the light when you are conditioned to living lies. Anne's nightmarish life of phobias had begun six years before when she became frightened first of reading, then of talking about anything that mattered. Soon her fears extended to touching metal, then to touching anything from the fridge, eventually a blind terror of receiving anything into her hands from anyone else. Her life became totally taken up with pills and visits to the psychiatrist.

Abroad, life became even more of a nightmare. There she had to attend social functions where every encounter terrified her. There was only one solution: more and more dependence upon strong anti-depressant drugs. Since she had such a terror of talking, reading or eating, doing so caused her heart to pound at a tremendous rate. This threatened her with the thing she most dreaded – a heart attack.

Anne had been a delicate child and had suffered recurring and severe attacks of pneumonia. Then had begun a morbid preoccupation with her physical condition. Also at the back of Anne's fears was the fact that her youngest daughter had been stricken with polio at six months.

The days that followed, while Anne stayed with us, were like being in the midst of a battle. Anne was fighting her way through to normality, and it took every bit of determination she had and all the support we could give her. Our daily, Mrs. Pryor, walked into the drawing room one morning to find Anne flat on her back on the floor, her feet up in the air.

"It's my blood pressure," Anne told her. "I have to do this."

"Oh, yes," said Mrs. Pryor, and came and told me. She was quite used to coping with any and every eventuality that arose in the course of her day at Post Green.

Anne's blood pressure was perfectly normal. Her mind and body exaggerated every symptom and caused her to think she was sick when she was not. I took her to be checked over by our family doctor, and he was able to tell her that none of the things she feared were true. She had been told this by doctors before, but now she was with people who were intent on helping her to re-establish herself in the truth – bringing God's light and his word to bear on her life. It was exactly as Jeanne and I had written in the leaflet "It's a Lie!"

We taught Anne how to use "scriptural prescriptions": that is to repeat to herself such scriptures as:

"If the Son liberates you – makes you free – then you are really and unquestionably free" (John 8:36, Amplified Bible).

"For God has not given us a spirit of fear, but of power and of love, and of a sound mind" (2 Timothy 1:7).

"I know whom I have believed and am persuaded that he is able to keep that which I have committed unto him" (2 Timothy 1:22).

"For God himself has said, 'I will never leave you or desert you', and so we can take courage and say, 'The Lord is my helper, I will not fear; what can man do unto me?' "(Hebrews 13:5,6).

We taught her to repeat these scriptures as a scriptural prescription three times a day: morning, noon and night. Jean had taught us the usefulness of such a discipline.

The most spectacular break-through came one evening as Jean prayed for her and Anne was filled with the Holy Spirit. God showed her then that her fear was not of sickness, but of death, and that she had been bound by this fear all her life. She saw that she had already died the only significant death there is, and had already passed into life.

Anne had a stong motivation to get well: she had a loving and understanding husband who needed her support and four children who likewise needed her. After this visit to Post Green, she made steady progress.

It had been the same with Nancy.

But Rosemary was different.

Looking back now I can see it was a matter of my will against hers.

Having Rosemary around was like having a tiger in the house. A slim, pretty, dark-haired girl in her early twenties, she had known love from many people, but she was determined to have it on her terms. The pressure that built up in her by her attempts to demand such a show of love from people caused her to get violently angry: she would slam doors, bang down china or pound a typewriter at a demonic speed.

She felt my love for her, but was insanely jealous of others whom she knew I loved just as much. One occasion when I took Bridget and Lizzie back to school, Rosemary drove the car. On the way home I urged her to drive faster, as I was late for an appointment and she was dawdling along the narrow Dorset lanes. Incensed at my wanting to hurry home, she put her foot down on the accelerator and the needle was soon reading 70 mph. We took the many corners on two wheels.

"Rosemary, stop!" I told her firmly.

By way of an answer she put her foot down further and the needle neared 80 mph.

I put out my hand and switched off the ignition. It was the only thing I could do. The car swerved into the hedgerow. Luckily we were not hurt.

Rosemary did change quite remarkably while she was with us, but she persisted in preferring her fantasy world of imagined love to the reality that was being offered to her. After six months, I arranged for her to go and live with friends near London. When she left she was more positive than I had ever seen her. She would have liked to have stayed at Post Green, but she knew that I would not agree to this. I felt the danger of her doing things just to please me – as I felt she probably was – rather than in obedience to God. She only stayed with our friends four months and then chose of her own volition to go back into mental hospital.

And Rudolph. While he was with us he had lived a fairly disciplined existence, but in the end he had decided he wanted to live an independent life. It had been his own suggestion that he should take a bed-sitter in Bournemouth. Once there he was quite erratic in his behaviour. We got used to receiving S.O.S.'s from Rudolph or from someone who had found him drunk – laid out on a park bench, or staggering around the back streets of Bournemouth. Tom and David would go and collect him and bring him home. Often he would be in a sorry state, and they would have to bath and change him.

For some reason or other Rudolph had never managed to put God first in his life. His love of good books and pictures, good music and fine living was more important to him. He was an upper-class Englishman who put culture and the way he thought God ought to be worshipped ahead of the reality of commitment and dedication to the Lord. Without such a commitment he could not walk free of the need to drink.

The fact that Post Green was beautiful and Tom and I were of the same background enabled him to change a few of his attitudes while he was with us, but when he was confronted with a person he found boring or whose manners were different, or we sang a hymn in a way he disliked, then he would get up and leave the room.

In the end he put himself into hospital again and had been there several months when he became seriously ill. It was discovered that he had a brain tumour, and he died within weeks. He knew the Lord and he had known we loved him, but it was a sad ending.

I wasn't sure about Carol. Certainly she had been healed and was now making her way in life; something she had not managed to do before. But there was something lacking; somewhere she wanted material things and her own way more than she wanted to follow God's directions for her life. It was the same as with Rosemary and Rudolph. It seemed that we could take them so far but no further. Was it their lack of commitment, or our lack of love? It seemed that we loved more than was humanly possible, but sometimes to no avail.

I did not doubt Kitty's commitment to the Lord, but she was still far from stable. It was with Kitty that we were to face the biggest crisis we had had since opening our home to care for people.

I was never as available to Kitty as she would have liked. None of us were. Increasingly our time was taken up with other things and other people.

As well as the monthly conferences, midweek teach-ins, summer camps, with all the preparations that these entailed, we had started to run small residential conferences: a "Roll-In" for young people over the Easter holiday, midweek conferences for ministers and full-time Christian workers. More and more Tom was talking about our having a "ministry to ministers". He had been elected a member of the General Synod of the Church of England and was continually in contact with ministers who wanted to know about our vision for church renewal. We were beginning to run training courses for church leaders and to produce study material for ministers to use in their own churches. All of this entailed more correspondence, more organisation.

Daphne had taken on a lot of the secretarial side of the work and she now had her office at Post Green (she and David were living nearby at Lytchett Matravers). Jeanne, along with helping with the cooking and counselling people, managed the organisation of the camps, residential conferences and training courses, and kept our accounts. We could no longer keep the money from sales of books and people's gifts in a paper bag or plastic container as we were wont to do: taking it like this to Cash and Carry to pay our next shopping bill. We were now dealing not just with fifty or sixty pounds each month, but more like five or six hundred.

We now had a full-time team which consisted of Tom and myself, Jean and Elmer, David and Daphne, Denis and Pinky Ball (Denis had given up both his part-time job with the gas board and his pastorate at the Elim Church in Bournemouth, and he and Pinky had come to live opposite us in one of the farm cottages), Rex and Betty Meakin, Jeanne, and Diana Cooper. Diana handled all the correspondence for Post Green Intercessors, people who had pledged prayer support. I had visited her the day I first spoke in tongues and she came to know the Lord as a result; she was now a radiant and firmly committed Christian, filled with the Spirit herself.

Some of us, such as Tom and myself, Rex and Betty and Diana, were able to support ourselves financially. The others were supported by gifts which came in at the meetings or through the post. As a team we met weekly to talk over what we were doing and to make decisions about the work. Already we were getting numerous invitations for members of the team to take renewal meetings around the country: Tom and David and Denis in particular. Elmer was busy with the Bible College and was not so available to travel. David, when he and Daphne had first moved down, had taken a part-time teaching job at the Manor School, but had now given this up.

Then there was the "area team" which had grown to some forty to fifty men and women – lay workers from nearby churches. They were mostly married couples in their thirties and forties, who met with us once a month for prayer, and who helped in the planning and running of the conferences and camps.

Jean's ministry had also grown. At the "Roll-In" she had shared the beginnings of an idea: that Christians should gather from all over the United Kingdom to take part in a mass demonstration in London – a demonstration for Christ and for Christian standards, standards which were being increasingly eroded by the growing permissiveness in secular society.

She had discovered later that she was not the only person to be impressed with such a vision: others too had begun to talk about such a happening. One by one they had heard about each other and the Festival of Light had become a reality. Now Jean was involved in helping to organise Jesus Festivals and other activities springing out of the Festival of Light.

With all this going on it was not so easy for Kitty, or others who felt like her, to slip into the house and spend a quiet hour with us, talking and relaxing together. Kitty had her friends around and about to whom she could go. She spent a lot of time with Jane and she was friendly with a good number of the area team, but mostly she wanted to spend time with Jeanne and me. It was not always possible. More and more she began to exhibit symptoms that were all too familiar: hysterical fits, anger, suicide threats. The fits were faked; Kitty had not suffered from epilepsy since the day Tom, Jeanne, David, Daphne and I had prayed with her. Finally the climax came when Kitty took an overdose.

It was not fatal, but to see Kitty beginning to go backwards again was more than I could bear. As far as I could I made myself more available to her. But it was never enough. The day came when Kitty attempted suicide a second time.

"She'll have to go back into hospital," Tom said to me firmly.

He meant mental hospital.

Back into hospital after she had been out of it for three years? She had proved she was able to hold down a job and able (more or less) to live by herself. I was not going to be so easily persuaded that that was necessary. But Tom was adamant. So was Jeanne. As the months had passed both of them had become more and more impatient with Kitty – and with me.

"I believe it's for her own good," Tom said.

I had talked often enough to other married women about the need to submit to one's husband: here was a hard test for me. It meant facing up to the fact that I had failed Kitty. I knew I must agree to what Tom suggested.

Tom was right: it was for Kitty's good. In hospital she went through the usual tests and interviews.

"But there's nothing wrong with you," she was told this time. "You can go home."

To be told by the hospital that she was well was an amazing testimony to Kitty – and to all of us. She only stayed there one week.

But where was home for Kitty now? Living by herself in a cottage in the village had obviously not been the right thing for her. Should she come back to Post Green?

"No," said Tom.

He had made up his mind that that would not be good for Kitty, or for me, or for any of us.

We contacted the Ponds, Kitty's friends near Andover, and talked the situation over with them. Yes, they said, they would be happy to have Kitty back living with them – for a period anyway. So Kitty went to the Ponds.

Kitty was healed. But I knew that she was not a totally whole person – yet. There were so many things that she still had to come to terms with. She truly wanted to follow the Lord, but she feared being committed to people. She knew that she needed to be, but she did everything to evade the issue. She feared being trapped by love; feeling safer if she could be just so close, but not too close. That was why in the end she preferred not to live at Post Green but had moved out to a caravan, then to the cottage in the village.

God had set her free from so many things, but she knew that she still had a long way to go. Who had failed whom? One thing was certain, it wasn't God who had failed – consistently as Kitty had taken steps of faith he had demonstrated his faithfulness to her.

The word "commitment" kept coming to mind. Somewhere I felt we weren't understanding it fully ourselves and this hindered us from being able to teach it to others.

Coming to terms with our failure to help Kitty any further, was one of the hardest spiritual paths I have ever walked. Jesus showed me his love as never before, and somehow he enabled me to forgive myself as I exposed my feelings of failure to him and saw how he identified with them by his seeming failure on the Cross. In this way he set me free of the guilt and pain of letting her down. With Kitty in Andover, I had nothing else to hold on to, but to accept forgiveness in its purest form, as only God can offer it – through faith and belief in Jesus Christ.

There were things Kitty still had to learn. There were things we had to learn too. But we had already learnt a lot. From the phone calls we received, it seemed we were further ahead than a good many others who were also concerned to have a similar caring ministry.

"How have you managed to deal with this problem?" callers would ask.

All went well for a while. Then relationships between the four married people became increasingly strained; for one thing they were not entirely agreed on how the home should be used.

When Ken and Val first visited Post Green they were just about at the end of their tether. It seemed to Ken that failure of some kind or other continually dogged his footsteps. Where was God in it all?

They came to join us for one of our monthly team gatherings. Jean was not always able to attend these meetings, but for once she was there. She was, however, tired and also a little dispirited. In fact, she was not feeling well and sat at the back of the room contributing little to the morning's sharing. That is, until Ken interrupted to ask us all to pray for him and Val.

They were strangers to most of the team, certainly strangers to Jean, who had not clapped eyes on them until she walked into the room that morning. This added to the poignancy of what happened next. That, and the fact that she was out of sorts herself. But Jean never said no to any promptings of the Holy Spirit; she was always available to him ("I just see myself as a waitress," is how she liked to explain the operation of the gifts of the Spirit). That morning as Ken spoke she had a strong urging to move from the back of the room and to pray for him and Val.

Jean began to prophesy, and as she did so she described in intimate detail Ken and Val's situation. For those few of us who knew, the atmosphere became electric; it was the most powerful operation of the word of knowledge that most of us had experienced. Jean ended by saying that the trouble lay in two trees planted too close together. The trees represented two totally separate callings; they needed to be separated and replanted, then each would flourish and bring forth fruit.

"The axe is laid to the root of the trees – not in judgment but in love," she continued.

Tears poured down Val's cheeks and swam in Ken's eyes as they received God's word. It reassured them that God had

14

One Word That Stuck

KEN AND VAL Ramsey were just such a couple. Ken was an Anglican clergyman; a worker priest. They shared their home with another married couple. For the four of them and for their families it was an experiment in community living, but not a very successful one.

Ken for a time had been a chaplain at Lee Abbey. He and Val met there. Married, they moved to South London and Ken took his first job in a factory – seeking to bridge the gap between church pew and shop floor. Few seemed to understand his reasons for doing this and he received little support. Ken was a "one man band" and not, he felt, a very effective one. It was some years before he met up with people who did understand and could encourage him – four French worker priests who lived and worked in the Portsmouth area, and Ken decided to move from London to Gosport in order to be closer to them (unfortunately they soon left the area).

As they prepared to move from London, a circular letter arrived from Lee Abbey. The letter asked several questions of past community members, such as, "Is there any value in community life as such, apart from any practical functions it might fulfil?" Ken and Val had often looked back to their time at Lee Abbey and wished that they knew of a way to transplant the kind of community life they had known into their ordinary life. As they considered the matter, they received a gift of money which enabled them to buy a sizeable house in Gosport. Friends of theirs, who had also been for a time with the Lee Abbey Community, were interested in forming a small community, so all four moved into the house together.

not forgotten or abandoned them, neither had they been entirely mistaken in believing that community was the path God had for them, but they had misjudged their timing and the outworking of this vision; not least, in that the four of them had different expectations.

"The trouble is we had no one really to help us sort that out," Val told Jean later. "We talked, but we didn't know the right questions to ask each other."

Ken and Val returned to Post Green a little later for a ministers' symposium and were both baptised in the Spirit. After some soul-searching conversations with their friends, the other couple moved away. Soon they had living with them a woman who had polio and who needed constant nursing. Two other single people moved in. Enthused once more to follow the vision God had given them, Ken and Val began to experience God using them in new and exciting ways. They were often on the phone or visiting, keeping us up-to-date. We visited them too. Soon their home had become a "mini-Post Green". God was using them to encourage others to receive the baptism in the Spirit, and using them too to pray for people's healing.

We saw the same thing happening with a farmer and his wife from South Devon. Constance Mundy came first to a series of women's meetings we were holding midweek. She returned later to a Saturday conference with a somewhat reluctant husband in tow. Hugh did not stay reluctant for long; soon he too was baptised in the Spirit. A retired army major, Hugh had survived a harrowing time in a prisoner of war camp during the Second World War. Thickset, jovial, a born leader, he was in every way the best kind of gentleman farmer. They came again as a family to Post Green, their two daughters, Lyn and Jo, were filled with the Spirit, and Hugh and Constance began to pray that their home might be used in much the same way as they saw ours to be.

It was exactly what we had always hoped for: that others would catch the same vision of opening their homes for God to use. Not necessarily all functioning in exactly the same way, but a home-based ministry where people could be drawn into and experience the family nature of the church.

But we had not anticipated the many questions that Ken and Val and Hugh and Constance would have. No sooner had they been baptised in the Spirit than people were flocking to them to ask questions, to request prayer, to seek healing. It had not happened quite so suddenly to Tom and me. We also had Edgar and Stephen and May and a good many others to whom we could turn for advice. How were these four to be helped?

There was, of course, Christian Life College, now numbering 120 students. Although the majority of the students were young single men and women there were some married couples among them; professional men who had given up good jobs to move to Poole and who had taken whatever employment they could get locally in order to support themselves and their families. But we could not expect that all those in need of such teaching would think it right to do this. Ken and Hugh were men already trained in the Church (Hugh was a lay reader and churchwarden) and the kind of teaching they needed was different to the majority of the C.L.C. student body.

I turned to Jeanne, certain that she could think up some solution. For a while between jobs as a youth leader she had worked with an organisation called The Navigators, which specialised in producing Bible study courses and in training Christian workers.

"Couldn't you come up with a course?" I asked her.

She was hesitant.

"You have to be pretty good to come up with things like that. And anyway if we look around we'll probably find that there are others already doing it."

I doubted it. The only course we knew of was one put out by a Roman Catholic Community in the States, the *Life in the Spirit* seminars. That didn't really meet the need: it didn't go far enough to help people like the Ramseys and the Mundys. But Jeanne hated to think of our doing things in an amateurish way and I could see that I was going to have to work hard to persuade her to put her mind to it.

In the end I got her to do so as a holiday task. She was going off to spend time with her family, and she went armed with *Life in the Spirit* as background reading, and strict instructions to come back with an outline of a course that we could put into action.

She did. Her idea was a course which dealt strictly with subjects which those thrown into the deep end like the Ramseys and the Mundys needed to know in order to teach others and to minister in the things of the Spirit. Subjects like the gifts of the Spirit, healing, deliverance, how to lead a prayer group and team ministry.

It was to be a course for leaders: those who could pass on their knowledge to others. The most important thing she felt about such a course was that home study should be backed by our personal involvement with people. Those enrolled could have notes, tapes and books to study at home, but they should come together every three or four weeks for a tutorial.

So we launched the Leadership Training Course – before we'd even got the material together. We settled on nine subjects: regeneration, baptism in the Spirit, gifts of the Spirit, healing, deliverance, prayer group leadership, some current errors, counselling and team ministry. It was to be a seven months' course; each section comprising three weeks' home study, followed by a tutorial at Post Green. Twice during this period we would draw people together for a weekend of fellowship and teaching.

Thirty-five signed on, including Ken and Val, Hugh and Constance.

As the course progressed, we produced the study material – usually only just in time, with members of the team compiling different sections.

We were developing a full-blown teaching ministry. With Kitty's departure a definite change of direction had taken place. It had not been obvious at first, but soon more and more people were commenting on the fact that the teaching was pushing out the caring. It was not strictly true, but the remarks hit home. Now we no longer had needy people actually living with us, our time was increasingly taken up with teaching and training.

People still came and were healed; a good bit of my time was given to talking to couples with marital problems, and we experienced God working in remarkable ways restoring broken relationships, healing hurts and disappointments. We rejoiced over those who came and went away with a new vision of how to minister in faith to those in need.

But a huge chunk of myself had been left behind. It was back there – with Kitty and Carol and Rosemary and Rudolph. Having them in the home had been what I liked. I fussed about it.

I griped at Tom and Jeanne, as though it was their fault which, in part, I probably felt it was. The day Jeanne flew at me and told me firmly to stop being so impossible, I knew I needed to take myself in hand.

"For goodness sake, Faith, you were the one to start us all off on this teaching lark," she shot at me, cutting across my moans. "Now either you were right in that, or you weren't. Can't you make up your mind and stick to it?"

We had been through all this so many times. Yes, we both believed that Post Green was called to a caring ministry as well as a teaching one. That didn't necessarily mean that it all had to take place at Post Green itself. For the moment, stretched as we were for office space and with everyone crying out for the kind of teaching we were supplying, it was necessary to cut back on having needy people staying with us – except for very short periods at a time. Perhaps this being so, others would be stirred into opening their homes.

Tom and I covered the same ground time and again. I knew it all. The only problem was that I didn't yet see many other people following our example. Oh yes, Ken and Val were, and Hugh and Constance, but strangely not those nearer home. They still seemed to rely on us.

"O.K.," I said to Jeanne, "I'll stop moaning – as from today." And I meant it. Outwardly, I could, and would.

That didn't mean I had stopped minding. In time, I was sure we would have such people living with us again.

Jeanne had renamed the dome. She now called it "the doom" instead. The name soon caught on. The dome had begun to dominate our lives. More and more meetings were held in it: some were gatherings for students from Christian Life College, but most were teach-ins and conferences that came around with alarming regularity. Anything going on in the dome spilled over into the house: people needed to use the toilets, and then they wanted tea and coffee and we would all be stumbling over each other in the kitchen.

This wasn't all. People had taken to driving in the gate at Post Green and doing a circle around the drive just to look at the dome. Strangers to us, they were in and around and out again. We might not have been a private home at all. That irritated us more than many other things.

The trouble was that the paddock faced the kitchen window; cooking or washing up we were daily confronted with "the doom" – like some strange object from outer space sitting in one's garden. But it had one big advantage: it was only a temporary erection. Tom, for this reason, particularly approved of it. It meant once God had accomplished what he wanted to do through us then the tent could be easily disposed of. There was a danger in thinking that God wanted a permanent centre established at Post Green. On occasions we talked about the possibility of building a hall or conference centre to house the meetings, but always we decided against this.

So the dome was a good thing really. It reminded us that God might change the direction whenever he wanted. But I doubted that his work among us was going to be so temporary, despite comments that we began to hear, such as "What's happened to the love at Post Green?"

We were having a hard time. I found a verse in Zechariah

that explained, at least to me, what we were experiencing. "In the whole land, says the Lord, two thirds shall be cut off and perish, and one third shall be left alive. And I will put this third into the fire, and refine them as one refines silver, and test them as gold is tested." (Zechariah 13: 8,9).

Tested we were certainly being, and with people questioning what was happening the best thing seemed to be to talk openly about it. I did so in our quarterly newsletter, which went to friends who had agreed to pray for and support the work.

"No time to love? That's what some say – is it true of Post Green? I expect so, often.

"Loving was easy when God started to work here, but now it is sometimes hard. Is it because we love less or is it because to love continuously is more demanding? As we see each other's faults it is pretty important to put what we preach into practice – to love, not to judge. We are having to learn that criticising is the quickest way to get into a muddle with the Holy Spirit, that forgiving has to be like breathing, that the devil has the best clippers for cutting communications, that hurt feelings are taboo, that what you think people are thinking probably isn't true, that trusting God is the best way.

"Being busy makes us tired – puts us under pressure – makes one snap – being snapped at makes loving more essential. No time to love? Never a moment that one dare not love."

Never a moment that one dare not love; I knew that to be true. We all knew it.

"At the moment I am using you in spite of yourselves. How much more then will I be able to use you when you are really one . . ." The Holy Spirit used Rex to speak this message to us.

Rex was less and less able to be with us at our weekly team meetings. Betty was dying of cancer, and it was distressing to see. We had come accustomed to Betty's gentle encouragement; a smile or hug from Betty and you knew that she understood everything that was going on, and that it was certain "to turn out alright in the end". Even now when we went to visit Betty she was the one to do the encouraging.

We prayed for her healing, but she did not get better. She died in August 1972.

We had encouragements, nevertheless. That summer we held our first Arts Symposium led by Merv and Merla Watson, Christian folk singers from Canada. This was preceded by our biggest event yet: a Festival of Praise with guest stars Judy Mackenzie, Merv and Merla, guitarist Gordon Giltrap, Liverpool poet Stuart Henderson, Pauline Filby and rock group Agape, a world-tour folk group from the U.S.A., and a student mime and dance group from London.

About 3000 people came that day. We had never had so many packed into the paddock and the praise spilled over the still summer air to be heard two miles off. We only had one complaint from nearby villagers; most seemed to enjoy the music, loud though it was.

Not all the comments that wafted back from the village community were so complimentary. A good many thought Tom and I had gone mad. Those, however, who had known us longest, remained loyal, but they were saddened not to see so much of Tom and me. Knowing they felt this way and not being able to do much about it, was unbearably hard for me.

That autumn we ran two Leadership Training Courses: a second one at Post Green, and another in London centred at St. Bartholomew's Hospital. Our pioneer course had been successful. It had not been easy for those taking part to complete the home study in such spare time as they had, but excited at what they were learning they kept at it. With each new subject the Holy Spirit opened up situations which enabled them immediately to put into practice what they were learning. Meeting together every three weeks we were knit together in such a way that all found it easy to open up and share with one another. Problems had been sorted out and lives changed as a result.

Now, in taking the course to London (at the invitation of a

graduate of Christian Life College; now a medical student at Bart's Hospital), we were doing so as a team: five or six people driving up to London every three weeks to take the tutorials. And earlier in the summer Jeanne, Daphne and I had been encouraged by attending the Fountain Trust International Conference at Guildford. Here we had been fascinated to hear Kevin Ranaghan, co-author with his wife of *Catholic Pentecostals*, speak of different phases that had taken or were taking place in the development of the Catholic charismatic renewal in the States. Much of what he said had a familiar ring.

He talked first of the *wildfire period*. In this period, he said, "scores of people are converted and filled with the Spirit, many are healed, all sorts of miracles happen.

"It's as though God is tapping us on the shoulder and saying 'Heh! Look here, I'm real. Let me show you my mighty power so that you may know I am.' Prayer meetings may start at seven in the evening and go on until two or three in the morning and the next day no one feels the worse for it. It's like a taste here and now of the kingdom that's coming."

Then he went on to speak of a second period: that of *casual or voluntary association*. He spoke of prayer meetings continuing to be a focal point, but getting shorter; of God dealing with people according to the regular pattern and rhythm of their lives; of their experiencing his power at work in their families and at their jobs.

People continue to desire to come together to pray and to worship God, he said, but they do so in order that they as individuals might be nourished and built up and strengthened, and that their needs as individuals might be met. This often led to prayer meeting hopping: people going where they were able to find the most benefit to themselves.

In this phase, he warned, the danger of individualism can lead to all kinds of deviant beliefs and behaviour and there is a need for sound pastoral leadership, solid and consistent teaching and a way of testing what goes on – in other words some form of authority. Where such authority emerges and functions properly groups grow stronger and become real spiritual oases.

This he told us was currently leading into a third phase of development.

"Many groups are beginning to experience the desire and the urging of the Spirit to become *permanent, stable communities*. To put it another way, individuals coming to groups have experienced a call from God to commit themselves to one another as brothers and sisters in order that they can share deeply – not just occasionally – the fullness of the Christian life.

"God is now calling together concrete manifestations of his body within which the full Christian life can be lived in a regular and stable way and as a result of which there is in a body – not just in scattered individuals – the fullness of the power of the Spirit operating regularly and consistently. And the result is a fantastic witness in a given area: the power of the Lord communicated, but in a humble down-to-earth and consistent sort of way."

The first two phases he had spoken of we could relate to; the third was still in many ways new to us. But I had a feeling that this was not to be for long.

He had used the word that was already on my mind a lot: *commitment*.

"God is calling people towards a deeper type of commitment that brings the charismatic renewal into every element of daily life and really brings it right down to ground level – to where we really live out our life," he had said.

One mid-November day, I was passing by the front of the house and noticed that the wind was catching at the entrance porch to the dome, causing it to flap. I called Jeanne and together we pinned it down. The wind was getting up, and I glanced over the dome to check that all was in order. It seemed to be, but I thought I would get Tom to take a look when he came in for supper. By the feel of things, we were in for a gale.

It was almost supper time anyway, and we had started the meal when Tom arrived.

"Quick," he shouted from the door, "the dome's taking off."

We rushed outside and saw that part of the frame had buckled, and the wind, which was now a good deal stronger, was getting under the terylene canvas and beginning to lift it: frame and all.

There was nothing the three of us could do alone. Jeanne and I rushed to phone for assistance. Within fifteen or twenty minutes a crowd of eager helpers had gathered. It was a matter of a salvage operation. The dome was edging its way across the field, the wind filling the canvas more and more. There was only one thing to be done: climb up the frame and cut the canvas down. That was a dangerous operation in the circumstances. When we had been erecting the dome, a young man straddling one of the steel struts had slipped and fallen, almost severing his thumb as it ripped on a sharp bolt.

That had been when the dome was stationary. Now we encircled it, clinging as best we could to the frame to keep it grounded, while volunteers swarmed up the supporting struts, knives in hand. To cut the canvas down was made doubly difficult because of the public address system strung across many of the struts. This had to be disentangled first. Whilst the bravest and most athletic were doing this, others crawled inside the tent and salvaged chairs, electrical equipment and the organ.

When it was all done and we stood or sat around the kitchen drinking tea, we drew breath and praised God that no one had been hurt and no other damage done.

Absurdly, we all felt at peace.

The next morning when the wind had died down and we could see the crumpled mess of steel frames and torn canvas straddling the paddock, I thought of the many who had given so sacrificially to help pay for the dome. What explanation could we offer for its loss? I thought of all those to whom it meant so much because of the memories it held for them.

The last series of meetings in the dome had been a series of teach-ins on divine healing culminating in a Divine Healing Day. There had been more people present on this healing day than at any previous conference. We had had to set out chairs in the drawing room again and relay the proceedings back to the house to provide an overflow meeting. The effect of the teaching preparatory to the Divine Healing Day had meant that many more people had come expecting healing and received it.

A lot of people would be sorry to hear that the dome had gone. But what was God saying to us? Perhaps it was an indication that after all the time had come for the work at Post Green to stop.

Jean was away on the continent at the time. The same evening the dome collapsed she had a vision. She saw waters gushing down from heaven; a mighty flood. As these waters reached the earth they met a rock-like structure and cascading down on either side of it began to spread out to irrigate the countryside around.

She received no interpretation to this vision, and did not know its meaning. Flying back home the next day, she was still wondering about it. But when she got back home and heard the news, she understood its significance.

The way God spoke to Jean confirmed thoughts we were already beginning to have. We had for sometime been talking about the need to decentralise the work; not to have everything centred at Post Green itself. Taking the Leadership Training Course to London rather than having the course members come to Post Green had been a step in this direction. Now we would no longer be able to hold big teaching meetings at Post Green; we would have to go elsewhere – into Poole or Bournemouth. Maybe use church buildings there. Inevitably, the loss of the dome meant the end of an era, and the beginning of another. Tom wrote in the newsletter: "We have always seen ourselves working for the renewal of the Church – the historic churches, and we believe the moment has come when we will see more churches proclaiming boldly that Jesus is alive. They will need encouraging, they will need teaching materials, they will need people to help them. I think that is the way forward for us."

Significantly, the newsletter which told of the loss of the dome was the first to be printed on our newly-acquired offset litho printing machine.

We had already begun to publish study materials for churches and fellowship groups, and these leaflets and booklets were printed by a local firm.

Jeanne not only wrote or compiled most of this material, she did the artwork and layout too – pasting it up on her bedroom floor – usually burning the midnight oil in order to keep to our agreed schedules

Getting it printed was costly; we could do it so much more cheaply ourselves – I thought.

When I first broached the subject, I was quickly shot down.

"Oh Faith, haven't we got enough to do without taking that on too?" was Daphne's comment.

Daphne was, undoubtedly, the most practical one among us. Over most things I valued her advice for this reason, but not over this!

It was a joke with Daphne that she preferred that Jeanne and I were never allowed to go off alone together – we always came back, she said, with a thousand and one ideas that meant a totally impractical work-load for everyone else. Sometimes she didn't mean it as a joke. Over the matter of doing our own printing, Jeanne agreed with Daphne, as did Tom.

I didn't get much help either from visitors who came and heard about the idea. My cousin Kenneth shook his head wisely and said, "Well, Faith, once you take that on you get into a different bracket altogether. It's a spiralling ladder, and not a very profitable one."

But, as always when I got hold of an idea, I couldn't let it go. I had seen a small printing machine being worked and was certain I could manage to run one very efficiently myself.

When I raised the matter for the umpteenth dozen time at one of our weekly team meetings and moaned that no one was taking me seriously, Jean intervened.

"I'll tell you what, Faith," she said, "why don't we pray and ask the Lord to supply a printing machine? If that is what he wants to do. We can't afford to buy one outright anyway. Having prayed, I suggest you let the matter rest."

I was willing for that – if everyone was going to pray in faith. *And* be willing to receive a positive answer, if it came. When I was fully assured that this was so, we prayed as Jean suggested.

It was only a little while later that Vic Ramsey, who had joined us again for the youth camps, said casually one meal time, "Do you know of anyone who wants a small printing machine?"

We named our printing works Faith, Hope and Charity Press. Laughingly, we explained to people that we called it this because I had to have the faith to work the machinery, Jean just hoped I could and Tom, during operations, needed all the charity he could muster! I enjoyed printing, but soon realised that it needed my total concentration. If anyone came into the print shop (a converted stable) while the machine was running I would bad-temperedly order them out again. People were not used to that with me. I could cook with a dozen or more people milling around the kitchen. To keep to Jeanne's deadlines, I often had to work late into the night. And even though I scrubbed my hands clean with soap and cleansing liquid, Tom still complained that I came to bed smelling highly of printer's ink.

These were things we could laugh about. Other matters were not so laughable.

Members of the area team (so called to differentiate it from the full-time team) were often complaining. When we met for team days one Saturday a month, there was still that same joy and praise and love – people enjoying the Lord and each other, and enjoying being involved in what God was doing; but I sensed an undercurrent of a different nature at work too.

Perhaps I sensed this because I knew what people were saying outside the meetings. They grumbled that they had been ousted by the "full-timers", that they were not kept as informed as they had been, that we did not listen enough to what they had to say. I wouldn't have minded this so much if they had come direct to Tom and me and shared what they were feeling. Then it would have been in the open and we could have sorted it out. But none of them did.

What was the good of our coming together to pray and be nice to each other when underneath there was a spirit of complaining and judging at work?

" . . . when you are one . . ." Rex had prophesied. I longed for the time when we would be.

People needed to share their grumbles openly and not go off and whisper in corners to each other. That word *commitment* kept rearing its head again and again.

15

We Can't Go to Bed Yet

HEARING KEVIN RANAGHAN speak at the Fountain Trust conference at Guildford gave me an idea. I still felt that Tom, Jeanne and I needed to be "one"; I believed this would precipitate a deeper unity in the whole team. But I didn't know how to get across to Tom and Jeanne my understanding of what it meant for us to be one. Whenever I thought about commitment, I found myself wondering about Tom and Jeanne's attitude to the work that God was doing among us: how committed where they?

How long would Jeanne stay with us? And Tom, if he had to make the choice between the work he did at County Hall and what was happening at Post Green, which would he choose? Tom was now not only Chairman of the Secondary Education Committee, he was also Chairman of the Education Finance Committee, and in charge of the committee's capital and revenue budgets. That meant he was handling a revenue of two million a year, and a capital budget of fourteen million. Career-wise, if one looked at it like that, he had done well, and he enjoyed it.

Then there was the subject that always caused sparks to fly between Jeanne and myself. That of her "being a member of the family". This is how I saw it, but Jeanne disagreed. When friends came to visit us, Tom and I always spoke of their being "welcomed into the family". Some were closer in than others, of course, but when Jeanne arrived we all – Tom and I and the children – felt she "belonged" in a special way. To me this was significant; the beginnings of something important that God wanted to do. But, somehow

I didn't seem to be able to get this across – to Jeanne, to Tom, or to anybody.

"Look at it this way, Faith," Jeanne once said to me when Kitty and Carol were living with us, "sometimes we're part of the family, and sometimes we're not. For instance, I come with you to Scourie each summer, but Kitty and Carol are not invited. At other times you and Tom and the children go off skiing or travelling on the continent, and I stay behind. Now if we were really one family there would be no picking and choosing between people even when it came to holidays."

We didn't invite Kitty and Carol to Scourie because that was the one time when we just flopped with friends and other members of the family, and I couldn't afford to allow a lot of disruption at those times – for other people's sake, as much as for my own. We did usually invite Jeanne to come holidaying with us on the continent, but she said she couldn't afford to do so, which was probably true, but also it was partly because she felt *the* family needed to be together on their own at times.

"So," she would go on to explain, "I don't mind when you go off to Switzerland, but I know it bothers Kitty and Carol. And they certainly don't like it when we all disappear to Scotland for five or six weeks in the summer. I really think it would be better not to say anything about our being part of the family because that would be more honest. Then people wouldn't get hurt."

I could see her point, but I couldn't agree. Sometimes I wished it did bother Jeanne more that the family went off at times without her. I wanted her to be fully one of us, and the barriers I felt were more on her side than ours. I was beginning to realise that it is hard for a mature single woman to give up her independence, as it is for a married couple to open up their relationship to include another person in it.

Having Jeanne in the home had certainly been interesting for Tom and me. It set up a totally different dynamic from having needy people around. She wasn't dependent on us, and she related as an equal. We were three mature people, but oddly the closer we got to each other the more immature our behaviour often was. With a third person around, Tom and I were made quickly aware of deficiences in our relationship – faulty ways of relating that we had long since accepted as the norm (because that made life easier for us), but which Jeanne now questioned us about. She didn't like me to appear to put Tom "down", neither did she like Tom venting his anger on me. We didn't like her being moody, and told her so. Living together was proving good for all three of us.

But we still had a long way to go. Then I had an idea. If I could get Tom and Jeanne to visit some of the places in the states that Kevin Ranaghan had spoken about at Guildford, then I felt sure we would return with a better understanding of what commitment to one another meant. Both of them were keen to go, so we began making arrangements.

Obstacles appeared.

Every February those who would be helping at our summer camps came together for a planning weekend. Early Saturday evening, after a full day of planning meetings, a few of us were preparing the evening meal at Post Green when Dot appeared in the kitchen. She and Roy had not long before driven home to get their evening meal, so I was surprised to see her there.

"Faith," she beckoned me urgently into the hall. I saw then how pale she was.

As I followed her, she turned and put her arm around me. "It's Bridget, Faith," she told me. "She and Adam have had a bad accident. They're being taken to Poole Hospital. Roy and I were just behind and saw it happen. I'm afraid Bridget may be badly hurt."

I was glad it was Dot breaking the news to me. She was such a stalwart and understanding friend. Heart in mouth, I rushed off to fetch Tom, and drew Jeanne aside on the way.

"Bridget's been in an accident. We need to go to Poole Hospital. Will you see to the supper and keep quiet about it until you hear from us. I don't want Grannie worrying while we're gone."

Then Tom and I were driving as fast as we could towards the hospital.

Bridget had been riding into Bournemouth on the back of a friend's motor-bike when they had collided with a car unexpectedly turning sharp right across their path. The force of the impact caused both Bridget and Adam to be thrown 40 feet, catapulted across the roof of the encroaching car. It was lucky that they were thrown clear because the motor-bike immediately went up in flames.

We knew nothing of these details as we entered the hospital, but we knew when we saw Bridget lying on a stretcher in casualty that her injuries were severe.

In the past, it had always been Bridget who had come rushing back to tell us of any accident that had befallen the others. Most often it had been Sarah who was in trouble ("Quick Mum, Sarah's fallen overboard!"; "Mum, Sarah's hit a car on the bend . . ."). Now it was Bridget herself.

She was conscious but hysterical with the shock and pain; her left arm was badly crushed.

"The surgeon's ready to operate on her arm right away," a nurse told us. "Do you give permission for him to do whatever's necessary?" Tom nodded, and signed the form she handed to him.

We were shown to a small reception room, and waited. On the way to the hospital, I had prayed one prayer over and over again: "She's your's, Lord. She's yours." I had been preparing myself for the worst. She was alive, but how bad were the injuries to her arm? I could not bear to think of Bridget handicapped in any way. The most naturally outgoing of all the children, she was also the most practical. She hoped to train as a nurse, and she would find it unbearably hard if this put an end to all her plans.

Eventually the surgeon came to tell us that he had done what he could. "But I'm sorry to say," he went on, "that I don't hold out much hope of her arm mending. At one point I thought I would have to amputate, but then decided I would rather take a look at it again later. For the moment

I've just cobbled it together; it was the best I could do. It might still be necessary to amputate. I doubt – whichever way it goes – that she'll ever have much use of that arm again."

"It's going to be alright, Faith." The surgeon gone, Tom's words cut across my panicky thoughts. The way he spoke I knew he was not saying this just to comfort me.

"I know it's going to be alright," he went on, "I can tell you I've been praying like stink. Like a fool I realised that I should have noted on the form that I did not want them to amputate without consulting us first. I told the Lord I was trusting him that Bridget's arm would be perfectly alright again. And I believe it – I have that confidence."

We looked at each other. What had the surgeon said?

"I thought I would have to amputate, but then I decided that I'd rather take a look at it again later."

It was a sign we much needed.

Adam had sustained fewer injuries than Bridget, but both would be in hospital for at least two to three months. As well as injuries to her arm, Bridget was badly concussed. As we continued to pray, we and others became even more convinced that God had the matter well in hand; indeed, that he was going to bring good out of the accident.

Bridget, once the worst effects of the concussion had worn off, was insistent that we go ahead with our trip to the States. Her arm was showing signs of knitting together, although the surgeon insisted that the amount of movement she would have would be small indeed. However, he was no longer talking of the need to amputate. Since Bridget was to remain in hospital, Tom and I decided to go ahead with our plans. But there was still another event to come before our departure.

This was an annual weekend when the area team came together for a time of prayer and of sharing. Always a guest speaker led the weekend: Bryn Jones, a Pentecostal minister from the north and a close friend, had been the first to do so; then Reg East. Now we had invited someone we had never met: the Rev. Graham Pulkingham, an Episcopalian minister from America.

He had come over to England at the invitation of the Bishop of Coventry to start a "community experiment" in a parish in the Midlands, and he had brought with him an extended family of eighteen; his own natural family numbering eight, and ten others from the Church of the Redeemer in Houston, Texas.

Graham was rector at the Church of the Redeemer; still was rector, although temporarily in England. We knew a little of his story – of the changes that had taken place at the Church of the Redeemer after he had been baptised in the Spirit in 1964; of the vision that God had given him at that time of the Church as a "community of brothers": men and women committed, at whatever the cost to themselves, to loving and serving one another and to meeting the needs of those God sent to them; of the phenomenal growth of that church as this vision began to be implemented and such a loving, serving, church community came into being. It was a notable success story; people travelled from all over the States – indeed from all over the world – to see for themselves the church that had pioneered a different kind of life-style and where they had heard miracles abounded. Michael Harper had written a book telling the story.

We – like others we knew – had conflicting feelings about an American coming to England to tell us how to live in community.

"English churches are very different to American ones. I would think we could probably teach community better than he," I foolishly commented to Jeanne and Tom.

I soon took back my words. I knew enough about God's ways with us not to presume any such thing. We were not a community anyway. I also knew that the Holy Spirit was grieved by such partisan talk. Our American friends did have a lot to teach us. We knew that better than some, since we benefited from Jean and Elmer's ministry among us. It would be good, I decided, for us to meet Graham Pulkingham, and for him to meet us. So we had invited Graham to take the area team weekend for us. He had written back saying yes. He would come and would bring a friend, Bill Farra, with him.

By now rumour about Graham Pulkingham abounded. He was gentle and unassuming, he was arrogant and rude; he was totally insensitive to people's feelings, he was the most understanding man that had ever been; he was totally uncaring of his wife and children, he was a family man.

What were we to believe? Should we ask him and Bill Farra not to come? Our team weekends were important to us all; perhaps it was not the time to have invited someone we had never met personally. But when I had suggested that we invite Graham, we had all been agreed about it. Once we had made a decision like that, I didn't think it right for us to change our minds.

As it was, I was in bed when Graham and Bill arrived, so my curiosity was not quickly satisfied. I had a heavy cold and wanted to be well for the next day's sessions. Jeanne cooked supper, and Tom entertained them with a long history of what had happened at Post Green.

"What's he like?" I wanted to know, when Tom eventually came upstairs.

"Very nice," said Tom. He got into bed and promptly went to sleep.

"Faith, do you love Jesus?"

It was the next morning and as we came into the drawing room where everyone was gathered for the first session of the weekend, Bill spied someone he knew (we had met at breakfast) and addressed me – in song.

I knew the song alright. I was meant to reply, "Yes, I love Jesus" (singing) and Bill would continue, "Why do you love Jesus?" and I would reply (again singing), "This is why I love Jesus . . ." and so on. Only I couldn't sing: everyone knew that!

So Bill tried it on the only other person he knew, Tom excepting. He tried it on Jeanne. Only Jeanne cannot sing a note in tune either. Both of us sat shaking our heads in confusion at Bill.

It was not a very auspicious start to the day. Neither did we make progress as the session continued. Graham seemed to be uncertain what to do. He read to us from the epistle to the Galatians, but then hardly commented at all on his reading. He just sat there, waiting; as though it was up to us to set the agenda for the morning. We were not used to this kind of leadership; normally our guest speaker would have come prepared with set teachings and have spoken for at least fifty to sixty minutes each session.

However, we could cope with most eventualities, and time passed as we questioned Graham, and he us. The problem was that Graham appeared reluctant to answer our questions about how things worked back at his church in Houston. He was more interested in questioning us. His questions came spasmodically and when they came they were not the ones we were normally asked.

"Who's the leader here?" he wanted to know.

We were through coffee-time by now and the morning was almost at an end.

Everyone knew the answer to that question.

"Tom and Faith," they chorused.

"Well, yes." He nodded, smiling.

Watching Graham, I attempted to sum him up. He certainly did not strike me as being arrogant or rude. And neither he nor Bill were the loudly-dressed, brash kind of Americans that one sometimes met.

"Let's see if I can put it another way," Graham continued. "Who makes the decisions?"

That was different.

"We all do," not so many voices now, but a good many. Tom and I were in on this one too.

"And," Graham was turning a pencil round and round thoughtfully in his hand, "who has the power of veto?"

Silence.

No one knew how to break the silence. Virtually everyone

in that room had the power of veto. I knew those who most often exercised it. This had put us in an awkward spot more than once; as a result we had at times made some bad decisions.

But I was not going to be the one to answer Graham.

"I think you know what I mean." He came to our rescue himself. "I'd just like you to think about it, that's all. Now who among you always knows everything that's going on, and always knows what needs to be accomplished?"

Again, there was silence.

"Faith." It was Dot who said it; she never minded speaking out.

People nodded; they knew it was true. But some were beginning to look a little embarrassed. This was hardly the kind of session they had been expecting.

"So who leads?"

I was beginning to get more the measure of Graham; this was hardly a man to trifle with.

"We all do," the same answer again.

"Oh," he said, "how difficult for you."

Again one could have heard a pin drop.

It was as well that it was lunch time. No one seemed to want the conversation prolonged. But I was excited; what Graham was onto I didn't know, yet I knew I trusted him.

One of the Bible college representatives, who had intended skipping the afternoon's meetings, went hurrying off to his lunch saying, "I'll be back after all." Although most people were on edge, no one wanted to miss what might transpire.

As the afternoon went on Graham continued his poking and prodding.

Why had we come together? what did we do? why did we do it? to what end? who decided what? (again); how did we resolve disagreements when they arose? no, he didn't believe there were no disagreements; did everyone always approve of Tom and me, of what we did?

Little by little, Graham prodded us all into speaking out. He opened "the whole can of worms": every bit exposed, the nice and the nasty. To me, it was a relief. This, I hoped, meant an end to all the "I-wish-they-had-told-me-before-they-did-it," and the "Why on earth did they do that?" behind people's backs. And before he finished, Graham had also shown fairly and squarely who *the* leader was: me.

I knew I was, but I would not have liked to have put it so bluntly. And there was still the question of the many who had the power of veto.

It was Jean Darnall who with her usual warmth and charm, leant forward in her chair at the end of the long afternoon's session, and said to Graham, "And what do you really think of us, Graham?" She voiced what many were wondering.

He smiled back at her and said quietly, but firmly, "I believe there is the potential in this room to convert all England."

He was not joking.

Sunday was more the type of meeting we were used to. Tom led a Bible study on "How to grow in faith", and talked about the need to speak your faith (even when you don't believe it!) believe your faith (even when you don't live it!); and live your faith, underlining our common need to belong to "an environment of faith" for this was a daily possibility.

Graham picked up what Tom said and talked about Abraham. The amazing thing about Abraham, he said, was that Abraham believed it when God told him that Sarah would bear him a son even in his old age. "Do you know why he was able to believe it? Because he was an entirely self-accepting man; he didn't doubt that God was speaking to him. And he was willing to look a fool; he was not a self-proud man."

Most of us, Graham continued, are not like that. We have been raised to be self-rejecting; to reject the deeper parts of our humanity. We are literally unable to accept ourselves, to accept our feelings and emotions as in any way trustworthy. So we missed a lot of what God is saying to us.

"Do you see," he said, "how contrary that is to a life of faith?"

He then went on to talk about Abraham pursuing the vision that God had given him.

"There are a lot of Christian dreamers," he said, "people who are not prepared to carry the burden of the vision. The burden comes when you are willing to do something to bring your vision to pass. Then the burden is the gift of God's grace to help you accomplish the vision.

"It's the vision plus the burden which equals a prophetic calling."

Here is a man who understands, I thought, as I listened to him; and I think he'd understand me, and the way I feel. Perhaps better than anyone else I've met.

But I wasn't sure about my willingness to bear the full burden of leadership; I sensed that few were willing to follow me. They were happy enough if they too could have a say in the decisions that were made, but if it came to trusting my decisions – or Tom's and mine for that matter – I wondered how many would be willing to follow.

The weekend's meetings over, I cornered Graham and talked to him.

"I don't know," I told him, "that I'm up to shouldering the kind of leadership you've talked about. Or that I want it."

He was standing looking out of the window, and didn't reply immediately. After a while he turned and said, "Then what happens, Faith, to the vision God has given you?"

I knew, unwilling as I was to accept myself as leader, that neither was I willing to lay down the vision that God had entrusted to me.

"Can you help us, Graham?" I asked.

He shook his head. "I don't know that I can. To be of any effective help I'd have to spend time with you all. Right now I'm in the middle of writing a book, and I feel the need to be with my family. I've been missing them and I think I owe it to Betty and the children to be at home for a bit."

I was sorry, but I was glad that he felt that way about his wife and children. That scotched some rumours I'd heard.

Jeanne also pressed him to stay.

"This is a good place to write a book," she said. But he refused.

"Well," she joked, as they got ready to leave, "now we know the worst, we needn't worry any more."

She then shared with Graham and Bill some of the ill reports we had received. He, kinder than she, did not tell us what he had heard about us, that we were a "wild pentecostal bunch, with a number of dominant women in leadership".

Women in leadership, he didn't mind; the dominant part he didn't like. And, as for "wild pentecostal bunch", that was not what he liked at all.

"I'd rather not go," he had told Bill, as the time for their visit drew near. "Let's write and cancel."

Bill had held Graham to the booking. Bill, a six-feet tall, lean Texan, had said little during the weekend's proceedings. A trained lawyer before he gave up his job to travel with Graham, his ability to sit-in-on-and-then-sum-up the proceedings was most remarkable; he never missed a thing and was equally aware of what had been left unsaid, as said.

As they drove away I knew that we had not seen the last of them.

"You know, Faith," said Jeanne, "seeing Graham and Bill together has done something for me. Somehow it makes more sense out of what has happened between us."

Jeanne had kept her word to me about accepting that our love for each other was God's gift. But it was still hard for us to share our lives so closely. A lot of people were critical of our relationship; they loved us both, but many wished we spent less time together. Yet that seemed to be what God wanted. Jeanne sensed that Graham and Bill had a similar relationship.

Two hours after he and Graham had left, Bill telephoned.

"We'd like to come back," he said. "In a few days' time. May we?"

They had talked over the situation, and decided that spending some time at Post Green was a priority.

The Church of the Redeemer was not on our U.S. itinerary. Inviting Graham to speak had been our one friendly gesture. But now Houston was included in our programme, and one or two other places that Graham and Bill suggested. After a few weeks we left them at home with other members of the team, and flew off to America.

Bridget was making progress, but unlikely to be out of hospital for at least another two months. We would be back well before then.

We started our trip in California where everything was large-scale (one hundred neatly blanketed cots row-upon-row lining the crèche of the First Baptist Church in San Jose); fast-moving ("This is hell!" yelled Tom, cajoled into riding the bob sleigh with Jeanne on the Matterhorn at Los Angeles' Disneyland); and a happier start to our trip we couldn't have had ("Dine here and have fun as well as food . . ." And we did).

"Things happen quickly in California," Ralph Wilkerson of Melodyland Christian Center (across the road from Disneyland) told us. Listening to him outline the Center's programme of teaching and training, caring and outreach, he might have been describing the ministry of Post Green, except in terms of growth and productivity there was no comparison.

"Yes, it takes us a little longer to get things going back home," admitted Tom.

In one thing we had the edge over our American friends. We realised this when we visited the home of Ken Pagard, minister of the First Baptist Church, Chula Vista. As the door opened in answer to our knock we literally stumbled into the midst of a closely-packed, strangely-staring, hands-extended circle of young – and older – people, all eager to shake our hands or give us a hug. They had never met an English baronet or a titled lady before!

The Baptist Church at Chula Vista was the first community household we visited, but from there on community faced us at every stop. We had not planned the trip this way, but the next church we visited was an Episcopal church in Miami

where the rector introduced himself to us and explained.
"The Lord's been talking to us about the need to be deeply
committed to one another. First, it was coming to know the
power of the Spirit. Then, learning how to be used in the gifts
of the Spirit. Now we're coming to understand that a vital
element undergirding all this is the concept of the body of
Christ – the family. For this reason, some of us have opened
up our homes to others in the church, and we have begun to
live as extended families."

The introduction to this church had not come from Graham
and Bill, and we had not heard beforehand about this development. Here we attended sharing sessions as those in newly-
formed community households talked over the problems
they were experiencing adjusting to such a different life-style.
Their problems were ones we knew; surprised, we were
coming to realise that we had already learnt a lot about community living without putting that label on it.

From Miami, we went to the Church of the Redeemer in
Houston. Then to another Episcopal Church in a black ghetto
area in downtown Detroit, where whites and blacks were living
together in community households, an unprecedented step
in that particular neighbourhood. Lastly we visited the mostly
student Roman Catholic Community at Ann Arbor in
Michigan. Increasingly we became aware of what God had
done at Post Green. Without our seeking or asking he had
given us the beginnings of community. As we went from place
to place what we saw and heard and felt was a reflection of our
own life back home.

But mostly it went deeper.

In the church communities at Houston and Detroit people
knew where they were with each other; their life was not only
purposeful (as ours was), but it was also peaceful (as ours often
was not).

"When I first came here, I wanted to get on and get things
organised," a lay elder at the Church of the Redeemer told us.
He was their business manager, overseeing the sale of records
and cassettes from the church's music ministry. "But I was

told that was not the way things worked here. First it was a matter of working out our fellowship together."

We discovered more about that as we sat in on their elders' meetings which often lasted all evening and on into the early hours of the next morning. No one went away with any unfinished business or unresolved feelings; everything was talked out; everyone was listened to. They were gentle with one another; no one spoke angrily, even though they spoke honestly.

"The way we relate to each other as elders of the community sets the tone for the whole church," explained Jeff Schiffmayer, priest-in-charge in Graham's absence. "Our commitment to one another and to the Lord is to see that we love each other perfectly."

We flew back home, but not straight home. We were booked to lead a tutorial day for the Leadership Training Course in Yorkshire. (Training courses were now being run in Yorkshire, in the Birmingham area, and in Norfolk, as well as in London.) From London Airport we went straight to Normanton, Yorks, where the monthly tutorials were held, and rested up for a day with Ray Smith and his family, Ray being the vicar of Normanton.

I was glad we were not going straight home, because I knew that Tom, Jeanne and I needed to do some serious talking *before* we returned.

About commitment.

"I can see that we need to learn to love each other perfectly," Tom said remembering Jeff's words to us.

Our talk about commitment had not got off to a good start. We had planned to meet immediately after lunch but Tom had gone off to mow Ray's lawn instead. It was the kind of thing Tom liked to do, but his commitment had been to meet with Jeanne and me.

I reminded him of this and not so gently either. "Why on earth did you have to do that now? You knew we were going to talk after lunch." Tom apologised. That over, we got down to business.

"I suppose for me it means not messing about as to whether I'm staying at Post Green," said Jeanne. "And working as hard at my relationship to you, Tom, as to Faith."

"And I can see I need to be as much committed to that as you," responded Tom.

Tom and Jeanne were alike in their reluctance to talk things out when needed. Unlike me they did not pursue the other – or anybody else – in order to put right any tiff or misunderstanding. Most often they left the pursuing to the other person.

"The trouble with me," Tom went on, "is that I need someone around reminding me continually of what I should be doing. Perhaps that ought to be your commitment to me, Jeanne."

"As long as you don't get angry when I do," said Jeanne, giving Tom a wry look.

Commitment among the three of us would mean all of this and more, we realised. But we understood better now that the quality of our fellowship was more important than any task.

On the basis of that understanding the three of us made a commitment – to see this kind of fellowship brought into being at Post Green – beginning with ourselves.

It was a first step: once back home, we talked to David and Daphne, Denis and Pinky, Jean and Elmer, Diana, Rex and Phyl (Rex had married again). Five (David and Daphne, Denis and Pinky, and Diana) felt it right to join us in such a commitment. Jean and Elmer, Rex and Phyl declined.

"I think I'm too old to take on any new commitments," Rex told us.

"Are you serious, Tom? Do you realise what you're saying?" Elmer asked bluntly.

He wanted to make sure that Tom and I fully understood the purport of what we were aiming to do. Unerringly, he and Jean saw further than others. They understood exactly what we were saying to them – that we were not just talking about deepening fellowship, but also if necessary a pooling of resources.

For Tom, as Elmer pointed out, that was no light thing. It had a number of implications. What about the estate? His inheritance?

"Yes, I know," said Tom, "but I mean it. What about you two?"

Sadly, Jean and Elmer said no. We were not surprised. Increasingly, Jean's ministry had been taking her away for weeks and months at a time. Just back from a trip to the States she was talking of bringing the Christian musical *Come Together* over to England from America. It would mean arranging concerts, organising on-the-spot choirs all over the country, appointing co-ordinators and music directors, co-ordinating publicity, planning the itinerary for the touring nucleus group, which was likely to include Pat Boone, as *compère*. It was too big an event for us to get involved in; our calling lay elsewhere. Elmer, moreover, had begun to talk of needing to have the Bible college more centrally placed: possibly in London, where employment would be easier to come by for the students. It was likely that our ways would part. It would be a while before this took place, but we knew the time would come when it would be right and necessary.

The commitment that the rest of us were making was to stay together in the expectation that it would be for life. We foresaw the possibility that God might call some of us elsewhere in time, but our expectation was that, for most of us, this would not be so.

"Let's give up and go to bed."
"No, not yet. We can't go yet."

Rex was wise in his decision not to join us, thinking that he would not be able to keep up the pace. The eight of us who came together to talk about commitment stayed up late a good many nights thrashing out our understanding of what a deeper commitment to one another meant in practical terms. We talked until 1 am or 2 am or later. It was the only time when we could be sure of being able to do so without interruptions. Our experience already was that it is usually at the point that issues become most crucial that interruptions happen; or it is time for bed.

Were we called to pool all our money and possessions?

Even maybe to move and to all live together under one roof? We agreed that in time God might call us – and others-to do this, and that we were willing for it to happen, but that this was not the first step.

"I believe, however, that such resources as Daphne and I have, need to be at the disposal of this group," said David. "That whenever and however a need arises among us we are committed to meet that need out of our own resources. In order that the vision that God has given us can be fulfilled. To feed England."

"And it means a commitment to say when any of us have a need; that may be harder," I added.

Primarily, however, we saw our commitment to be a commitment to love one another, not to hide from each other – our needs, joys, sorrows, complaints, grudges, but to learn to live in open and perfect fellowship with one another; as perfect as was possible by God's grace working in each of us. This fellowship would be the basis for the continued growth of the caring/teaching work at Post Green.

For the eight of us, it meant also sharing leadership. As a result of Graham's first visit, I had fully accepted that God had entrusted to me his vision for Post Green. Now that I was certain that the other seven were as committed as I to seeing this vision fulfilled this leadership could be shared; together we were "guardians of the vision".

Hours were spent taking "the vision" apart and putting it back together again. Not used to talking quite so freely and openly to one another and never having had time enough before we now discovered differences and misunderstandings even among us; and we were the inner team. We had to be agreed, and this didn't mean glossing over disagreements or refusing to listen to someone else's ideas when they contradicted our own. We wanted to learn to hear the Lord in one another: to presume that when one of us spoke, the others heard the Lord speaking. That meant we thought twice about speaking too lightly, or presumptuously.

We learnt more of what David and Daphne were feeling. Both of them felt able now, in the light of the commitment we had made, to say how they had often felt insecure being on the outside of Tom's and Jeanne's and my relationship. They knew they were committed to the three of us, but they were not sure of our commitment to them. Now having heard us actually voice such a commitment Daphne felt free for the first time to ask questions and to share her thoughts, even if they contradicted what the three of us were saying.

What a lot we were learning about each other! Denis hating to be pinned down to meeting at a regular time, but willing to do it; Pinky, who usually said even less than Daphne at team meetings, now opening up and sharing herself with us; Diana, unable to believe that our commitment to her meant a commitment to her family and all the difficulties that were hers as a widow with three young children, yet wanting to believe it; and Jeanne, Tom and I willing to share with the others the problems we had faced and were still facing in working out our relationship with each other. Open too to hear too what they had to say on this.

All these were but steps towards drawing others in. Those who would be prepared to voice the same kind of commitment-to the Lord, to us and to the work God had established. In order that the vision might be fulfilled. "To feed England," as David had said.

"Let's not go too quickly," said Jeanne. "We don't know what commitment to each other means yet, let alone to a wider group."

But we would learn.

16

Postscript

TWO YEARS LATER, on the 3rd May, 1975, the Post Green Community officially came into being. On that day the Bishop of Salisbury presided over a Service of Commitment in Lytchett Minster Parish Church at which forty-two of us stood and publicly made a prayer of commitment.

> O God, who has called us in Christ
> to be partakers of this commitment to one another,
> we engage ourselves in love for you and one another,
> to work out this commitment
> in harmony with your perfect will.
> We are no longer our own but yours.
>
> I am no longer my own but yours.
> Put me to what you will;
> rank me with whom you will;
> put me to doing; put me to suffering;
> let me be employed for you or brought low for you;
> let me be full; let me be empty;
> let me have all things; let me have nothing;
> I freely and heartily yield all things
> to your pleasure and disposal.   Amen.

"The vision of the Post Green Community," David had said earlier in the service, "is to create an environment where people who have committed themselves to the Lord Jesus can work this out in a loving commitment to one another in such a way that the Holy Spirit can fully use his gifts in their lives. We believe God has called us to be a teaching community and that this should issue out of our common life. Our aim is to teach thoroughly the few who will in turn teach others. Our desire is the renewal of the Church through the power of the Holy Spirit.

"Working out this loving commitment means learning what it really means in practical ways to lay down our lives for each other. To make love our aim. To meet together regularly to study the word, to pray and to worship the Lord, and then to pass on to others what we are learning. For some of us, it will mean living together, for all of us a larger measure of sharing our lives with one another."

Reg East, who preached at the service, also talked about commitment. He spoke from his own experience of community life at nearby Whatcombe House (Reg and Lucia now had their own conference centre run by a small resident community). "We have to learn that we are committed to people as they are, not as we would like them to be," said Reg." This involves a realism which for most of us is the most demanding thing in our lives. We have to be stretched, we have to receive new ideas, our prejudices have to be knocked for six, and our emotional weaknesses are sometimes mercilessly exposed.

"I don't think," he continued, "we can really learn to love until we are willing to be hurt. And it is not until we learn to love that we begin to savour the really deep, rich things that belong to the human personality.

"Living together is a painful experience, but it leads us through to a deeper sense of a life diffused with joy and richness. The loveliest things of the human personality can come to birth - and surprisingly, in oneself.

"It is growing together in love that matters, not how many gifts the Holy Spirit bestows. They are only there for the outworking of the love of God. It's not when things are going easily and smoothly that the love of God flows. It's when we are coming to grips with each other and it's very hard, when the bottom seems to have fallen out of our community life and someone or other is badly hurt, but nevertheless we are determined that we shall love. It is when this is going on that the Holy Spirit does shed the love of God among us, and people see it."

The Service of Commitment was another new beginning. The months that followed, as we attempted to keep each other to the commitment we had made, were some of the most difficult we had yet been through. We had said that we wanted to live a common life, but there were areas where each of us retained the right to make his or her own decisions without reference to the others. These areas differed from person to person and this made the situation even more complex. It soon became obvious that "every man did what was right in his own eyes". This verse from Judges was a good commentary on our community life. The step we had taken had not caused this to happen; it had merely revealed to us the truth about ourselves. Some of us went back time and again to Graham Pulkingham to ask his advice. Sometimes we took it and sometimes we didn't.

Over the months since we had first met Graham and Bill, they had been able to help Tom, Jeanne and me to work out the dynamics of our relationship. Graham with his wife, Betty, and with Bill, had been through all the same difficulties we had as a married couple and a single person seeking to open our lives in depth to one another. They knew it was important for the three of us to understand what God had done among us, and why: that family is not something that is structured, it is born of love, that it was necessary for our marriage to be opened up to a third person or persons (not of our natural family) for the wider family at Post Green to come into being.

We were a family, but there were many things that we still could not work out. We still had not come to grips with the problem of leadership. We believed in a shared leadership, but what did this mean? There are many different ways of sharing leadership. Where in the end did ultimate authority lie? Were we meant to be a completely democratic institution with every member having an equal say? We had among us people at varying levels of spiritual and emotional maturity; this aggravated the problem.

In an attempt to decide these issues we began to work out a more defined structure, ignoring Graham's advice not to run our life on such lines. "Rules and regulations are not what it's all about," he stressed.

The fact that we all loved each other dearly, but still had these difficulties, made our life more, not less, painful. "You need to get your life together, or cease living this way. If you don't, some of you are going to get hurt badly," Graham told us.

While this was going on, Bridget went to live with Graham and his family and became temporarily a member of the Community of Celebration (so-named, October 1973), at first living in Coventry and then at Yeldall Manor in Berkshire. Physically on the mend, emotionally she was still raw. We watched the deep healing that took place in her as she drew from the life of that community. This gave us even more reason to trust Graham's judgment.

Our path didn't begin to level itself out until we committed ourselves to take Graham's advice Doing that brought our community and his closer. In January 1976, eleven members of the Community of Celebration (from the Isle of Cumbrae in Scotland) moved to Post Green and became members of Post Green Community. Others followed. They brought their considerable experience in pastoral care and community living with them.

As our lives intermingled with theirs and theirs with ours so the two sides of the Post Green ministry came together again: the caring side and the teaching. Post Green is no longer the only household to carry the burden of ministry, whether teaching or caring. There are now many households involved.

The two communities remain separate, but are closely linked. There is quite a bit of coming and going among members of Post Green Community and members of the Communities of Celebration in Scotland, in Berkshire,

England, and in Colorado in the United States – as there is between these communities and other associated communities in the United States and elsewhere; communities with a similar life-style.

We each have our own distinctive ministry: all serve the cause of church renewal – but we are one family.

As we see the church is called to be.